GUIDE TO
EGYPT

MICHAEL MARCH

Highlights for Children

CONTENTS

On the cover: The world–famous ancient pyramids with a camel caravan in the foreground

The publisher is grateful for the assistance of Theresa Musacchio, a graduate student in Egyptian studies at the University of Pennsylvania, who reviewed this book.

Published by Highlights for Children
© 1995 Highlights for Children, Inc.
P.O. Box 18201
Columbus, Ohio 43218-0201
For information on *Top Secret Adventures,* visit www.tsadventures.com or call 1-800-962-3661.

10 9

ISBN 0-87534-916-1

EUROPE

ASIA

Egypt

AFRICA

AUSTRALIA

ANTARCTICA

△ **The Egyptian flag**
The red and black
bands and the eagle
represent Egypt's
struggle to become a
republic. The white
band represents a
bright future for the
country.

EGYPT AT A GLANCE

Area 385,229 square miles (997,739 square kilometers)

Population 80,000,000

Capital Cairo, population of city and surroundings 15,750,000

Other big cities Alexandria (population 4,000,000), Port Said (554,757), Aswân (241,261), and Luxor (422,407)

Highest mountain Mount Catherine, 8,652 feet (2,637 meters)

Longest river Nile, the world's longest river, 4,160 miles (6,690 kilometers); section crossing Egypt 650 miles (940 kilometers)

Largest lake Lake Nasser, 2,300 square miles (6,000 square kilometers)

Official language Arabic

▽ **Egyptian stamps** Some of the pictures on these stamps depict artifacts from Egypt's glorious past. Others show that today Egypt is a modern Islamic state.

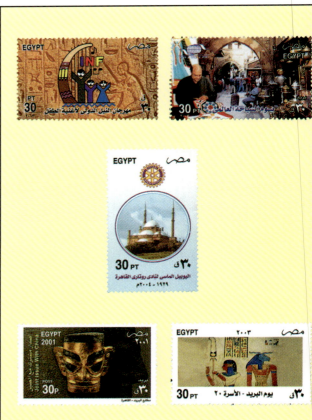

◁ **Egyptian money** These are two Egyptian banknotes. Egypt's currency is based on the Pound, written as £E. There are 100 piastres to the pound.

4

MEDITERRANEAN SEA

Nile Delta

WEST
BANK

GAZA
STRIP

ISRAEL

JORDAN

Matrûh

Rosetta

Alexandria

Port Said

Zagazig

Suez Canal

Giza
CAIRO
Memphis
Saqqara
Maidum

Faiyum
Oasis

Suez

30°N

Qattâra Depression

Siwa Oasis

Sarabit
el-Khadira

Sinai
Peninsula

Mount
Sinai
Mount
Catherine

Dahab

SAUDI

ARABIA

Western Desert

Bahariya
Oasis

Nile Valley

Gulf of Suez

Gulf of Aqaba

Farâfra
Oasis

Hermopolis
Tell-el-Amarna

Asyût

Red Sea

Hurghada

L I B Y A

Qena

Karnak

Luxor

Thebes

Mountains

25°N

R   E   D

S   E   A

Idfu

Kôm Ombo

Darâw

Aswan
High
Dam

Aswân

Philae

Tropic of Cancer

25°E

Lake
Nasser

Abu Simbel

EGYPT

Farmland

Desert

★ Capital

● Major Cities

▲ Mountain Peaks

∴ Ancient Ruins

— Country Boundary

0   25   50   75 Miles

0   50   100 Kilometers

S U D A N

30°E

35°E

N

W   E

S

20°N

© Oxford Cartographers

5

THE GIFT OF THE NILE

Egypt is located in the northeast corner of Africa. It is a large country—about as big as Texas, Oklahoma, and Arkansas put together. Nearly all of this land is hot and dry.

Most of Egypt is desert. In the spring, dusty winds, called *khamseen*, blow across the country from the Sahara Desert. In the summer temperatures are very hot—usually 95° to 100°F (35°–38°C). In spite of its harsh climate, people have lived here for thousands of years. They have survived because of the Nile River. The world's largest river brings fresh water and life to the desert.

The river flows from south to north across Egypt. For centuries the Nile has flooded, leaving rich soil along its banks. People farm along the fertile river valley.

The Nile splits into many branches as it nears the Mediterranean Sea. This region is called the Nile Delta.

▷ **The Sphinx and the Great Pyramid** The Sphinx was built to honor Khafre, the son of Khufu, a pharaoh who lived nearly 5,000 years ago. These monuments are located at Gîza, near the modern city of Cairo.

◁ **Faiyûm Oasis in the Western Desert** Water holes like this are rare. The Faiyûm's water comes from ancient canals linking it with the Nile. Palm trees, cotton fields, and orchards grow here. Faiyûm Oasis is located 50 miles (80 kilometers) from Cairo.

△ **A boy by the Nile in the desert** He wears a light-colored, loose head covering, shirt, and long robe to keep cool in the hot climate.

One of the world's oldest civilizations grew up on the banks of the Nile. More than 5,000 years ago, great kings called pharaohs ruled here. They built palaces along the river. Many ancient monuments are still standing.

Arabs became rulers of Egypt around A.D. 640. Today Egypt is an Arab republic with a president instead of a king. Most Egyptians are Muslims — followers of the Islamic religion.

Air-conditioned trains run between Egypt's cities. You can get to smaller places by bus. You can travel up the Nile in comfort on a cruise ship, or step back in time and hire a *felucca* — a traditional Arab sailboat.

For the tourist, Egypt offers much to see and do. You can visit ancient temples and palaces, take a camel ride across the desert, buy gifts in bustling markets, and scuba dive to explore coral reefs teeming with fish.

CITY OF VICTORY

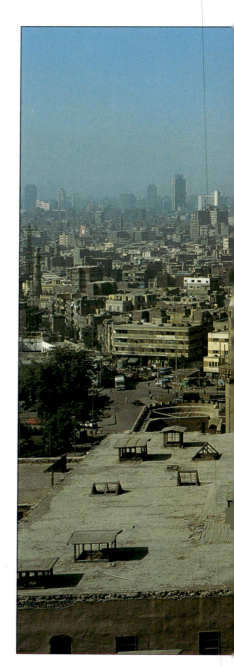

Egypt's historic capital, Cairo, lies on the Nile River, at the tip of the Nile Delta. It is the largest city in Africa. More than a fifth of Egypt's population live here. The country's government is here, too. People say that anything important that happens in Egypt happens in Cairo.

Cairo was built over thousands of years. Its name comes from the Arabic word *al Qahira*. It means City of Victory. Some parts of the city existed long before the Arabs came here. A carved pillar of stone that was built by the pharaohs about 3,000 years ago still stands in one northern suburb. The buildings in Cairo show how the city has been ruled. There are more than 1,000 mosques in the city. But there are also Roman ruins next to modern skyscrapers, museums, and office buildings.

Traveling in Cairo is not difficult, but the buses can be very crowded. Traffic jams on the streets are common. It is easier to travel by minibus or taxi or to take the subway. The subway station names are written in English and Arabic. Many sights are a short walk from the center of the city.

Bazaars and markets are exciting places to shop. You can buy traditional goods, such as copper and brass coffee sets, gold and silver jewelry, wooden chessboards, and tapestries. Here, the shops and market stalls do not have fixed prices. You must bargain for what you buy. Begin by offering about half of what you want to pay.

Cairo has many restaurants. You can try a variety of Egyptian dishes, such as *ful medames* (mashed beans served with lemon juice and spices). You can also eat Greek and many other foreign foods such as Mexican and Indian.

▷ **The crowded skyline of modern Cairo** The pear-shaped domes of the mosques contrast with the modern skyscrapers.

▽ **Fruit and vegetable market** Egypt's fruits are among the best in the world. They include oranges, figs, melons, apricots, and mangoes.

▽ **Crowded buses in the Cairo rush hour** Buses are packed with riders—inside and out.

MUMMIES, MARKETS, AND MOSQUES

The Egyptian Antiquities' Museum in Cairo is world famous. Here you will find thousands of priceless objects from the time of the pharaohs. These include statues, vases, jeweled ornaments, and paintings.

The highlight of the visit is the vast collection of treasures from the tomb of Tutankhamen. King Tut, as he is often called, was nine years old when he became pharaoh. He died at the age of eighteen.

When a pharaoh died, people removed the inner organs from the body. They used special mixtures and bandaged the body to keep it from rotting. The process is known as embalming. The ancient Egyptians put the body, or "mummy," into a set of beautifully decorated coffins. These were placed in a stone coffin called a *sarcophagus*. They laid the sarcophagus in a tomb along with the pharaoh's treasures.

◁ **The al-Azhar Mosque** The tall towers are called minarets. From here, the *muezzin* calls Muslims to prayer.

▽ **Beaten-gold innermost coffin of Tutankhamen** The boy-king is made to look like Osiris, the ancient Egyptian god of the dead.

▽ **A Cairo street scene** The arched gate of the *Bab Zwayla* is at the end of the street.

The Khan el-Khalili is the best-known shopping district in Cairo. The bazaars sell everything from silks and gold jewelry to perfumes and spices. Behind the shop fronts, people are busy in their workshops. They hammer metal, dye cloth, and carve wood to make the goods they sell. You can approach the Khan from a crowded narrow street called the Muski. But be careful as you go!

Men pushing carts shout out warnings as they hurry through the street. Traders sell salted fish and water flavored with licorice.

The al-Azhar Mosque and University are nearby. You must take off your shoes before going into the mosque. The university was founded in the year A.D. 971. It may be the oldest university in the world. Students from many other countries come here to study.

11

FORTS AND PYRAMIDS

Old Cairo, or Misr-el-Qadeema, is one of the oldest parts of the city. This district was founded by the Persians when they invaded Egypt nearly 2,500 years ago. In about A.D. 100, the Romans built a fortress here. The fortress has wide circular towers. At that time, some of the first Christians lived in Old Cairo. Christians in Egypt today are known as Coptic Christians. They have their own Bible and their own churches. The lovely "Hanging Church," built over the old Roman fort, is a marvelous place to visit.

The Pyramids of Gîza stand on the west bank of the Nile. The pyramids contain the royal tombs of some of the pharaohs and their queens. If you like climbing, you can explore the royal burial chambers.

The Great Pyramid is the biggest of all. It is 480 feet (147 meters) high and 755 feet (230 meters) square. The Great Pyramid was built nearly 4,500 years ago. It is made from more than two million big blocks of stone. The stones fit together so well that you cannot squeeze a knife blade between them. To this day, no one knows how the ancient Egyptians managed to build anything so huge.

The Sphinx, the large statue with the body of a lion and the head of a man, is another puzzle. It is at least as old as many pyramids, but no one really knows when it was built.

Memphis, the ancient capital of Egypt, is about 20 miles (30 kilometers) to the southwest of Cairo. Not much of Memphis remains today. There are more tombs of pharaohs nearby at Saqqâra. The huge Step Pyramid of Djoser, the oldest pyramid of all, is also there.

◁ **Cairo's Muhammad Ali Mosque** This beautiful building stands inside the walls of the Citadel. This fortress was built by Saladin, ruler of Egypt in the 12th century A.D.

◁ **The Step Pyramid of Djoser** It was designed by the pharaoh's chief architect, Imhotep. He began the age of pyramid building around 2630 B.C.

▽ **The Manial Palace, Rôda Island, Cairo** The building mixes Western and Eastern architectural styles.

EGYPT'S BACKBONE

Farmland is very scarce in Egypt. Most lies either in the fertile strip of the Nile Valley or in the Nile Delta region. About two-thirds of the people here work on the land. The farmers are called *fellahin*.

Ever since Egyptians first settled on the banks of the Nile, the fellahin have been the most important workers in the country. They once depended on the river bursting its banks and flooding the valley. The floods occurred in summer. When the water drained away, it left mud and sand behind, making the land fertile. The Nile flooded its banks nearly every year. When it did not, the farmers faced a serious problem. They could not grow enough food to feed Egypt's people.

To solve this problem the Aswân High Dam was completed in 1970. The dam and many canals provide the water the farmers need. Even so, many farmers still use ancient methods for lifting water from the Nile onto their land. Some villages have water piped to each house. In other places, people have to do their washing in the river.

It looks as if life has changed very little over the centuries. Flat-roofed, brightly painted mudbrick houses are clustered around narrow roads and alleyways. Chickens, goats, and water buffalo wander freely. Pigeons are kept in coops for their meat. From an early age, girls learn to cook, bake bread, and feed the animals. Boys are taught to build houses, plow, sow seeds, and harvest crops.

Farmers have grown wheat in the Nile Valley since the days of the pharaohs. They have also grown sugarcane since medieval times, but the most important crop is cotton. (Egypt sells much of its cotton to foreign countries.) Beans, rice, and potatoes also grow in the Nile Valley.

▷ **Old and new farming methods**
For hundreds of years, fellahin have used oxen to pull plows. With the help of the government, today's farmers can use modern machinery like tractors.

▽ **Camels in a desert town** Camels are used to carry goods in the desert.

◁ **Two fellahin by an irrigation well** Some farmers still use animals to drive simple machines to get water from deep within the earth.

TEMPLES AND TOMBS

Qena is a small town in southern Egypt. Aswân is Egypt's southernmost city. And between Qena and Aswân, there are more ancient monuments than anywhere else in the world.

The ancient city of Thebes was once the capital of Egypt. Most of it is buried beneath the modern city of Luxor. At the heart of this dusty place, you will find the dug-out ruins of a great temple. It was built by the pharaoh Amenhotep III. Pharaoh Ramses II later made the temple bigger. Its towering gateways were once plated with gold. The walls were covered in marble with gold and silver decorations. The temple is more than 3,000 years old.

Nearby is the Avenue of Sphinxes. This wide pathway is named for the stone statues that stand along its sides. The avenue once connected the temple of Luxor with the Karnak Temple. Today only part of it remains.

It took about 1,300 years to build the Karnak Temple. Within this walled temple is the Temple of Amun. It has high gateways, a massive hall with rows of stone columns, and huge stone statues.

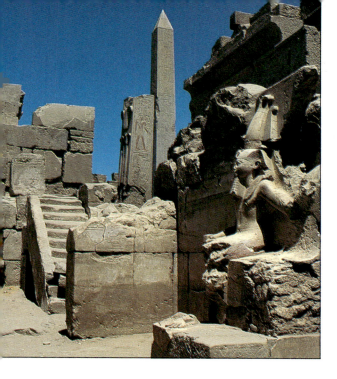

◁ **The Obelisk (center) of Queen Hatshepsut** It is located at the Temple of Amun in Karnak. Hatshepsut was Egypt's only female pharaoh.

The pharaohs of Thebes were buried on the opposite bank of the Nile. They were hidden away in rock tombs in the Valley of the Kings. It was hoped that their tombs would be safe from robbers. Sadly, most of the tombs were robbed of all their treasures long ago. You can visit the royal tombs, including Tutankhamen's tomb.

The old town of Kôm Ombo lies about 100 miles (160 kilometers) south of Luxor. The ruined temple here contains mummified animals such as crocodiles. Nearby Darâw is famous for its camel market.

◁ **Camel market** Buyers and sellers gather for the day's business. The camels are brought to Egypt from Sudan. Young animals are sold for riding or to carry cargo. Older camels are sold for meat.

▷ **Ancient temple at Luxor, by the Nile** The temple was discovered in the 1800s under 20 feet (6 meters) of rubble. At the back of the site, on the right, is the mosque of Abu el-Haggag.

MONUMENTS OLD AND NEW

From Aswân town, you can hire an Arab *felucca*, or boat, to take you across to the west bank of the Nile. A short uphill ride on a camel brings you to the beautiful ruins of the Monastery of Saint Simeon. It was built by Coptic Christians.

Aswân, like Kôm Ombo, is the home of the dark-skinned Nubians. Their ancestors lived at the same time as the pharaohs. In fact, some of the later pharaohs were Nubians themselves.

Much of the old Nubian homeland now lies under water. When the Aswân High Dam was built across the Nile in the 1960s, the valley behind the dam was flooded. A huge man-made lake formed. Gamal Abdel Nasser was president of Egypt at that time, and the lake is named after him. The Aswân High Dam took ten years to build. It is the largest in the world. The dam controls the amount of water flowing along the Nile Valley, so that farmland does not dry up. The dam also has giant turbines that are turned by water and provide much of Egypt with electricity.

The Temple of Abu Simbel is Egypt's largest temple. It is probably also its finest one. It was built by Ramses II in about 1240 B.C. The temple now stands on the banks of Lake Nasser. This huge sandstone monument was cut up into blocks and rebuilt on higher ground in 1968. This was done to save this ancient treasure from the rising waters of the lake. The Temple of Isis was also moved from Philae to another island.

▷ **An Aswân village** Houses of mudbrick and wattle (woven sticks and branches) are crowded around a dusty square.

▽ **Island near Aswân** A *felucca* passes Elephantine Island in the Nile River. The Agha Khan's tomb stands on a distant hill on the west bank of the river.

◁ **The Temple of Abu Simbel** Four statues of Ramses II, two of which are seen here, were built at the temple site. They are all 65 feet (20 meters) high.

CITY BY THE SEA

Alexandria is Egypt's biggest port. It sits on the Nile Delta and the Mediterranean Sea. The city is named for Alexander the Great who conquered Egypt in 332 B.C. He gradually turned the small fishing village here into the country's capital. Alexandria is still Egypt's second-biggest city after Cairo, the modern capital.

Alexandria is a popular seaside resort. The city has lovely beaches and cool sea breezes. In the summer, people come to escape the heat of the Nile Valley.

Alexander the Great was a Greek from Macedonia. The city named for him still serves the best Greek food in Egypt. It is also known for its seafood. Grilled shrimp with lemon is a local favorite.

▷ **Fort Qait Bay overlooking Alexandria's eastern harbor** The fort stands on the site of the old Pharos Lighthouse, one of the famous Seven Wonders of the Ancient World.

▽ **A caleche driver with his passengers** Touring Alexandria in a *caleche*, a comfortable horse-drawn carriage, can be fun.

▽ **A street scene in the center of Alexandria** Many of the buildings date from the 1800s and look very European in style.

From 304 to 30 B.C. Egypt was ruled by a series of kings, all called Ptolemy, and their queens. They made Alexandria a great center of culture and learning in the ancient world. The Ptolemies built palaces, a museum, and a world-famous library. The last of these rulers was the famous Queen Cleopatra.

A Roman theater, discovered less than fifty years ago, is one of the few ancient buildings left in the city. The semicircular arena is made of layers of brick and stone. It seated about 800 spectators.

The town of Rosetta (or Rasheed) is on the edge of the Nile Delta to the east of Alexandria. In Rosetta, in 1799, French soldiers from Napoleon Bonaparte's army found a stone covered with both Greek words and hieroglyphs. *Hieroglyphs* are the picture signs used as writing by the ancient Egyptians. The "Rosetta Stone" made it possible for experts to translate, or decipher, ancient Egyptian writing.

DESERT SAFARI

Far out in the Western Desert, near Egypt's border with Libya, is the little oasis town of Sîwa. An oasis is an area of the desert where the ground is wet and fertile. At Sîwa there is both fresh and salt water. Date palms grow here. In summer the heat is fierce. Winter brings chilling winds to the town.

▽ **A cobra** There are snakes living in the Nile Valley as well as in the desert.

Sîwans have their own customs and their own language. The women cover themselves in robes from head to foot. They wear heavy silver jewelry. Sîwans consider silver more valuable than gold.

If you look south from a hill near the oasis, you see the Great Sand Sea reaching into the distance. The huge sand dunes are beautiful but dangerous. About 2,500 years ago, the Persian army tried to cross this desert. These soldiers were never seen again.

The desert oases were beyond the reach of tourists until recently. Today, buses run between most of the oasis towns. Much of the desert you cross is not sand but gravel-covered plains. The rocky White Desert, which is between Bahariya and Farâfra Oases, magically changes color. It appears white at dawn, then turns golden, and finally purple at night. Plants grow around the oases, but you are unlikely to see crocodiles, ostriches, or other animals there.

Bahariya and Farâfra both have hot-water springs, where you can bathe. Farâfra is tiny. The people of this desert village earn their living by selling their crops of dates and olives in distant markets.

Dakhla and Kharga, to the southeast, are much bigger and more built up. Kharga lies on the old Forty Days Road. This was the route that was once taken by slave traders. They crossed the desert with their camels from Sudan on their way to the Nile Valley.

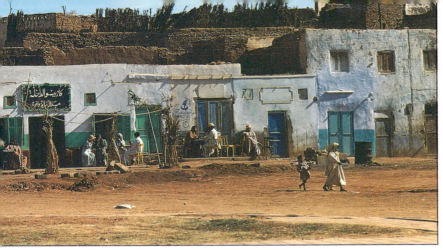

◁ **Mut town at Dakhla Oasis** The pace of life is slow and the people are very friendly to visitors.

▽ **Dakhla Oasis** By using irrigation, Egyptians reclaim land from the desert for farming.

GATEWAY TO ASIA

Near the modern town of Zagazig, in the eastern Nile Delta, lie the ruins of Bubastis. Bubastis was founded about 4,000 years ago. It was named for the goddess Bastet. In Egyptian art and sculpture, Bastet is often shown as a cat. The Egyptians were the first people to domesticate cats. Some cat owners even mummified their pets when they died.

During the reign of pharaoh Ramses II, workers dug a canal close to Bubastis that linked the Nile River with the Red Sea. Later rulers reopened and extended the old canal. Egypt became the gateway for trade between the Mediterranean and Asia.

Today, the Suez Canal links the Mediterranean directly with the Red Sea without the help of the Nile. The modern canal was built by Ferdinand de Lesseps, a French engineer and diplomat. Digging began in 1859. The work was not completed until 1869.

De Lesseps lived at Ismailia. You can still visit the large house that was his home. Like Ismailia, the waterfront town of Port Said was built around the time of the canal. Port Said stands at the northern end of the canal at the entrance to the Mediterranean. In its early days, it was a den of smugglers. Today, much of the town is rebuilt. It has become a popular summer resort.

At the southern entrance to the canal is the city of Suez. It was once the center of the old spice trade with Asia. Since the Middle Ages, Muslim pilgrims have passed through here on their way to the holy city of Mecca in Saudi Arabia. Oil refineries and chemical plants ring the modern city. Farther down the Red Sea coast is Hurghada. At this popular resort scuba divers explore beautiful coral reefs.

▽ **Suez Canal** Every day, up to ninety ships pass through the 100-mile (160-kilometer) man-made waterway.

◁ **Port Said** The town was damaged during a war with Israel in 1967. It has since been rebuilt, but has much of the character of an old port.

△ **Seashells for sale at Hurghada** The resort lies on a bay that has a coral island at its center. Here, colorful shells cover the seabed. All kinds of fish from the bay can be seen in Hurghada's aquarium.

HOME OF THE BEDOUIN

Most of the people who live on the Sinai Peninsula are Bedouin. The Bedouin were Arab tribes who pitched their tents around the oases. Throughout the year they roamed the desert in search of plants to feed their sheep and goats. These fierce and proud people counted their wealth by the number of camels they owned.

The Bedouin make up only a tiny part of Egypt's population. Their nomadic, or roaming, way of life is slowly disappearing. Today many Bedouin are settled. You will more often see them driving a taxi or truck than riding a camel. Some also work as tour guides. They lead camel expeditions or Jeep safari parties across the craggy wilderness of southern Sinai to remote village oases.

▽ **A Bedouin father with his children** Many Bedouin families in Sinai now live in stone huts rather than in goatskin tents.

▽ **Mount Catherine** It takes five or six hours of hard walking to reach the summit of Egypt's highest mountain.

△ **Bedouin making coffee at Feiran Oasis, near Mount Sinai**
The Bedouin are good hosts, but guests who stay too long are as welcome "as the spotted snake."

Saint Catherine's Monastery stands beneath Mount Sinai. Moses is said to have heard God speak to him from a burning bush in this valley. The monastery is home to Arab mosaics, illuminated manuscripts, and other priceless works of art.

The way to the monastery from the ancient turquoise mines leads through Wady el Raha Pass. Nearby there is a sacred tomb. Every summer, on the Prophet Muhammad's birthday, the Bedouin gather for a *moulid*, or festival, at this tomb. They rub tomb dust on their bodies for good luck. They also race camels and feast on roast camel stuffed with lamb.

The Gulf of Aqaba, on the east coast of the Sinai Peninsula, is a marvelous place for underwater swimming. Here you can explore the fantastic coral reefs in clear waters crowded with brightly colored tropical fish. There can be no better way to relax at the end of your tour of the beautiful and ancient land of Egypt.

EGYPT FACTS AND FIGURES

People

Most Egyptians are of mixed race. They are descended from the Arabs and also from the ancient Egyptians, Berbers, Greeks, Turks, and other races. The Nubians, in the south of Egypt, are a largely separate people with their own language. The Bedouin, who live on the Sinai Peninsula and in mainland deserts, are mostly of Arab descent.

Trade and Industry

Oil from the Gulf of Suez and Sinai makes up about half of Egypt's exports. Tourism and tolls on ships using the Suez Canal also bring in money from abroad. The cities of Cairo and Alexandria are the main industrial centers. Factories and mines produce phosphates, coal, manganese, iron, steel, and aluminum.

Cotton is Egypt's most important export crop. Egypt and Sudan together grow one-third of all the cotton in Africa.

Egypt has to buy about two-thirds of its food supply from other countries and needs to borrow money from abroad.

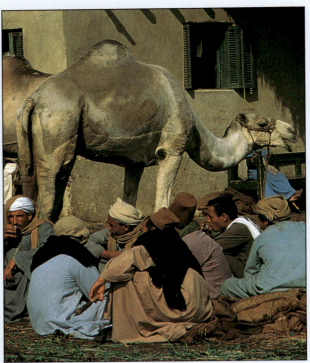

△ **Imbaba camel market, Cairo** Here, twice a week, camels are bought and sold or exchanged for sheep and goats.

Fishing

Egyptians fish in the Mediterranean Sea for fish, shellfish, and squid. However, since the building of the Aswân High Dam across the Nile, there have been fewer fish to catch. This may be because the dam has affected sea currents along the coast. Lake Nasser has been stocked with fish. Freshwater fish also live in the Nile Delta lagoons. Deep-sea fishing in the Red Sea is popular.

Food

The Egyptian people eat more *ful* than any other kind of food. Ful is a kind of broad bean. Egyptian popular dishes include:
Ful medames: the beans are cooked and served with olive or corn oil, lemon juice, and spices.
Tameya: deep fried and seasoned ful patties. They are served in pita bread with salad and pickles.
Shish kabab: grilled pieces of meat, which are usually served with a spicy sauce and pita bread.
Hummus: a paste made from mashed chick-peas. It is often used as a spread.
Sharwama or *Shawermah*: thin slices of pressed, roasted lamb flavored with seasoning, eaten in a sandwich.
Hamam: pigeon, either grilled and served with wheat stuffing, or stewed with onions, tomatoes, and rice in an earthenware pot called a *tajine*.
Umm ali: bread pudding in milk, with coconut and cinnamon.
The Egyptians like tea more than any other drink. They like it strong and very sweet. Coffee is served strong, without milk, and sweet or bitter (without sugar).

Farming

Only about four percent of Egypt's land is suitable for farming. Lake Nasser, behind the Aswân High Dam, now provides water all year round so that crops can be harvested two or three times a year. The dam has also made it possible to irrigate, or water, large areas of desert that can be used for farming.

The use of modern chemicals has led to better harvests, especially of cash crops, such as cotton. Most cotton is grown in the Nile Delta, which has the richest farming land. Only about a quarter of the land is used for growing food. Rice, maize, wheat, beans, millet, and dates are among Egypt's major food crops. In some regions, olives are an important crop and source of income for farmers.

Farmers also grow potatoes, tomatoes, other vegetables, and all kinds of fruits. Some of this food is sold to other countries. Most farmers also keep water buffalo or dairy cattle. These animals can pull a plow or turn a waterwheel as well as provide milk.

△ **Wall painting from Horemheb's tomb in the Valley of the Kings** The pharaoh is shown with the goddess Isis.

Schools

Children go to school between the ages of six and twelve. There are free state schools, as well as private schools and religious schools. After elementary school, children take an exam before going on to intermediate school. They can then, if they wish, enroll in a secondary or high school. Afterward, some continue their education at one of the four state universities or many colleges.

The Media

The state owns all radio and television stations. There are 8 television channels. One shows western movies and has daily news in English. The others are in Arabic, and one of them is broadcast only to Cairo.

There are about 15 daily newspapers. The oldest is *Al-Ahram* (The Pyramid). *Mayo* is the newspaper of the government. *Egyptian Gazette* is published daily in English and French.

Art and Drama

Ancient Egyptian sculptors used all kinds of materials as well as precious metals. They made wood carvings using yew, acacia, and sycamore. Painting, on the walls of temples and tombs, was bright and colorful. It followed the rule that the heads of the figures, but not the eyes or the shoulders, were shown in profile. Modern Egyptian art includes carpets and tapestries featuring designs in silk and wool.

Egypt's most famous actor is Omar Sharif, star of the well-known films *Lawrence of Arabia* and *Doctor Zhivago*.

EGYPT FACTS AND FIGURES

Music

Egyptian music is different in each region. Horses are trained to dance to *sa'idi*, the music of the Nile Valley. Sa'idi uses the *naharsan*, a kind of drum. *Fallahi* comes from the Delta area, *sawahlee* from the Mediterranean coast. Nubian music reflects various African styles.

Religion

Islam, the religion of the Muslims, came to Egypt with the Arabs in A.D. 640. Muslims believe that Muhammad, a man born in Mecca around A.D. 570, was the final prophet of God. Muslims pray five times a day, and fast throughout *Ramadan*, the ninth month in the Muslim calendar. The *Koran* is their holy book. Many Muslims perform *Hadj*, a pilgrimage to the holy city of Mecca in Saudi Arabia, at least once in their lifetime.

Festivals

Muslim festivals and *moulids* can be huge gatherings. At the center of many is the *zikr*, the honoring of God, through prayer and by the reciting of the *Koran*.

△ **A female mummy** From about 2900 B.C. the bodies of dead kings and queens were dried out and bandaged to preserve them.

Some important festivals are:

Ramadan During this month, Muslims fast from before dawn until after sunset. A three-day holiday called 'Id al-Fitr follows.

Moulid al-Nabi (in July or August) Muhammad's birthday is an occasion for street processions in many towns and cities.

'Id al-Adha A celebration to honor the Prophet Ibrahim's willingness to sacrifice his son in obedience to God's command.

Plants

Papyrus, a plant used to make the first form of paper, was once common along the banks of the Nile. Now it grows only in the extreme southern part of the country. Grasses and mimosa shrubs grow in some desert regions. Date palms grow in the oases and the Nile Valley.

Animals

Birds of the Nile Valley and Delta include turtle-doves, bluethroats, redstarts, stonechats, as well as water birds such as ibises, storks, and the great crested grebe. Birds of prey include falcons and kestrels. The Nile crocodile grows up to 14 feet (4 meters) long. Wildcats and mongooses live in the Delta. Gazelles, hyenas, jackals, scorpions, and all kinds of insects live in the desert. Snakes include the deadly carpet viper and the Egyptian cobra.

Sports

Soccer is Egypt's national sport. Horse races and camel races take place in the desert. Tourists enjoy scuba diving, snorkling, and deep-sea fishing.

HISTORY

Stone Age people lived in Egypt 250,000 years ago. By 4000 B.C., two kingdoms had grown up—one in the Nile Valley (Upper Egypt), the other in the Nile Delta (Lower Egypt). About 3100 B.C., the two kingdoms were united under the ruler Menes. For most of the next 2,500 years Egypt was ruled by kings called pharaohs. The pharaohs built a great empire and conquered neighboring countries. In 525 B.C., the Persians invaded Egypt, followed by the Greeks, and then the Romans, who became Christians. In the 7th century A.D., Egypt was conquered by the Arab rulers from Damascus, who introduced Islam. Later, the Fatimids from North Africa invaded and built Cairo as their capital. In 1171, Saladin, who spent most of his time fighting the Crusaders, became ruler. By the 1500s, Egypt had become a province of the Ottoman Turks. World War I (1914-1918) ended the Ottoman Empire, leaving Egypt with its own king but under the control of Britain. In 1952, a group of Egyptian army officers seized power, declaring Egypt a republic. Colonel Gamal Abdel Nasser became the country's first president in 1956 and ruled until 1970. Egypt gained control of the Suez Canal from Britain in 1956. Two wars with Israel followed, in 1967 and 1973. The Israelis seized Sinai, but President Anwar Sadat, Egypt's leader from 1970 to 1981, made a deal with Israel for its return. Sadat was assassinated in 1981. His place as president was taken by Hosny Mubarak.

LANGUAGE

Egypt's official language is Arabic. Arabic is spoken by most of the people of North Africa and West Asia. The spoken language can differ from country to country, but the written language remains the same.

Unlike English, Arabic is written from right to left, and has its own alphabet. Although Arabic was brought to Egypt from outside, some people think the Arabic alphabet was developed from the signs of ancient Egyptian hieroglyphic, or picture, writing.

Useful words and phrases

English	Arabic
Zero	*sifr*
One	*wahid*
Two	*ithnayn*
Three	*talaata*
Four	*arb'a*
Five	*khamsa*
Six	*sitta*
Seven	*sab'a*
Eight	*tamanya*
Nine	*tes'a*
Ten	*'ashara*
Sunday	*youm il-ahad*
Monday	*youm il-itnayn*
Tuesday	*youm al-talaat*

Useful words and phrases

English	Arabic
Wednesday	*youm il-arb'a*
Thursday	*youm il-khamees*
Friday	*youm il-gum'a*
Saturday	*youm is-sabt*
Good morning	*sabah il-kheer*
Good evening	*masa' il-kheer*
Good night	*tisbah 'ala-kheer*
Please	*min fadlak*
Thank you	*shokran*
Yes	*aiwa/na'am*
No	*la*
Can you speak English?	*titkalim ingleezy?*
Excuse me	*'an iznak*

INDEX

Note: Many Egyptian words have more than one spelling. For example, *Ramses* is often spelled *Ramesses*, and there are several correct spellings for names of foods.

Acknowledgements
Book created for Highlights for Children, Inc. by Bender Richardson White.
Editors: Lionel Bender and Peter MacDonald
Designer and make-up: Malcolm Smythe
Art Editor: Ben White
Editorial Assistant: Madeleine Samuel
Picture Researcher: Madeleine Samuel
Production: Kim Richardson

Maps produced by Oxford Cartographers, England.
Banknotes from Thomas Cook Currency Services.
Stamps courtesy of Scott Publishing Co., Sidney, OH 45365 (www.scottonline.com).

Editorial Consultant: Andrew Gutelle.
Guide to Egypt is approved by the Egyptian Government Tourist Office, London.
Consultants: Muna Abdoon, Library of Congress, Cairo, and Mohammed M. Aman, University of Wisconsin, Milwaukee.
Managing Editor, Highlights New Products: Margie Hayes Richmond

Picture credits
ESTO = Egyptian State Tourist Office, LION = Lionheart Books, Z = Zefa. t = top, b = bottom, l = left, r = right. Cover: Z. Pages: 6, 7l: Z. 7r: ESTO. 8-9: Z. 9tl: ESTO. 9tr: Z/Olive Sawyer. 10l: Z/A. Pasieka. 10r: Z/F. Damm. 11: Z. 12: LION. 13t, 13b: Z. 14: LION. 15t: Z. 15b: Z/K. Scholz. 16, 17b: Z. 17t: LION. 18b: Z/Vontin. 18-19: Z/F. Damm 19t: Z/Bert Leidmann. 20l: ESTO. 20-21, 21t: Z/F. Damm. 22: Z. 23t: Z/K. Geobel. 23b: Z/K.Scholz. 24: Z/F. Damm. 25l: Z/Sunak. 25r: ESTO. 26l: Eye Ubiquitous/Paul Stuart. 26-27: Z/Werner Braun. 27: Z/Havlicek. 28: Z. 29: Z. 30: Z.

The Joy of Spring

A collection of impressions recognizing the inherent joy and beauty in reawakening Nature.

ACKNOWLEDGMENTS

"Actually, spring invites participation . . ." by Hal Borland. From the book SEASONS by Hal Borland. Copyright © 1973 by Hal Borland. Reprinted by permission of J. B. Lippincott Company. "This is the time of year . . ." by Hal Borland. Reprinted by permission of Curtis Brown, Ltd. Copyright © 1964 by Hal Borland. Excerpts from SIGNS AND SEASONS by John Burroughs, Copyright 1886, 1895, 1914 by John Burroughs. Published by Houghton Mifflin Company; excerpts from OUR NATIONAL PARKS by John Muir, Copyright 1901 by John Muir, Copyright 1909 by Houghton Mifflin Company; excerpts from THE WILDERNESS WORLD OF JOHN MUIR by Edwin Way Teale, Copyright 1954 by Edwin Way Teale; excerpts from BIRDS AND POETS; LOCUSTS AND WILD HONEY; RIVERBY; WINTER SUNSHINE; LITERARY VALUES; LEAF AND TENDRIL; THE SUMMIT OF THE YEAR all used through courtesy of Houghton Mifflin Company. "The most precious things in life . . ." by John Burroughs. From JOHN BURROUGHS—BOY AND MAN, edited by Dr. Clara Barrus. Copyright 1920 by Doubleday & Company, Inc. Reprinted by permission of the publisher. The following excerpts: "One of the new pleasures . . ."; "Nearly all the warblers sing in passing . . ."; "Bird-songs are not music . . ."; "The casual glances . . ."; "The close observation of nature . . ."; "If I were to name the three most precious resources . . ."; by John Burroughs. From WITH JOHN BURROUGHS IN FIELD AND WOOD, edited by Elizabeth Burroughs Kelley, © 1969 by A. S. Barnes and Co., Inc. Excerpts by Susan Fenimore Cooper. From RURAL HOURS, Copyright © 1968 by Syracuse University Press. "April" from SILVER IN THE SUN by Grace Noll Crowell. Copyright 1928, 1934 by Harper & Row, Publishers, Inc. By permission of the publisher. Excerpts by Annie Dillard from PILGRIM AT TINKER CREEK by Annie Dillard. Copyright © 1974 by Annie Dillard. By permission of Harper & Row, Publishers, Inc. Excerpts abridged from THE BEST NATURE WRITING OF JOSEPH WOOD KRUTCH. Copyright © 1947, 1949, 1962, 1964 by Joseph Wood Krutch. By permission of William Morrow & Company. WET-WEATHER TALK and WHEN THE GREEN GITS BACK IN THE TREES by James Whitcomb Riley. From THE BEST LOVED POEMS AND BALLADS OF JAMES WHITCOMB RILEY, Copyright 1920, The Bobbs-Merrill Company. Specified excerpts: "Days sped by in an agony . . .", "The regularity with which . . ." from THE WORLDS OF ERNEST SETON, edited by John G. Samson. Copyright 1976 under the International Union for the Protection of Literary & Artistic Works. Published by Alfred A. Knopf, Inc. Specified four excerpts: "It was late May . . ."; "How much good the rain would do . . ."; "I forgot my work . . ."; "Spring in the north . . ." from SIGURD F. OLSON'S WILDERNESS DAYS, by Sigurd F. Olson. Copyright © 1956, 1958, 1961, 1963, 1969, 1972 by Sigurd F. Olson. Reprinted by permission of Alfred A. Knopf, Inc. Specified five excerpts: "To anyone who has spent . . ."; "The song of the robin . . ."; "Early morning in the wilderness . . ."; "A meadow lark sat on a fence post . . ."; "I have always believed . . ." from THE SINGING WILDERNESS, by Sigurd F. Olson. Copyright © 1956 by Sigurd F. Olson. Reprinted by permission of Alfred A. Knopf, Inc. HEPATICA by Henrietta Staege. From CREATIVE WISCONSIN, Spring 1959. Used by permission of Mary H. Staege. Excerpts by Edwin Way Teale. Reprinted by permission of DODD, MEAD & COMPANY, INC. from THE AMERICAN SEASONS by Edwin Way Teale. Copyright © 1950, 1951, 1956, 1957, 1960, 1965, 1976 by Edwin Way Teale; reprinted by permission of DODD, MEAD & COMPANY, INC. from NORTH WITH THE SPRING by Edwin Way Teale. Copyright 1951 by Edwin Way Teale; reprinted by permission of DODD, MEAD & COMPANY, INC. from CIRCLE OF THE SEASONS by Edwin Way Teale. Copyright 1953 by Edwin Way Teale. Our sincere thanks to the following author whose address we were unable to locate: Stephen Wright for NEW ENGLAND STONE WALLS.

PHOTO CREDITS

Alpha Photo Incorporated, 17; Camerique, 68 (top); Bruce Coleman, 1, 6, 12 (top), 37, 45, 56 (top), 64 (bottom); Colour Library International, 36; Ed Cooper, 5, 9, 40, 42, 46, 52, 55, 56 (bottom), 80; Ken Dequaine, 16, 25; A. Devaney Incorporated, 18, 29 (top), 33; Freelance Photographers Guild, cover, 24, 48; Olive Glasgow, 44, 60 (bottom), 61; Hampfler Studios, 13 (bottom); Grant Heilman 3, 7, 8, 10, 19, 20, 31, 32, 38, 39, 49, 50, 60 (top), 62, 63 (2), 64 (top), 65 (top), 66, 70 (top); Image Bank, 28 (bottom); Harold M. Lambert, 14; Luoma Photos, 22; Frank Miller, 21; Josef Muench, 51; Laura Riley, 68 (bottom), 70 (bottom), 72; H. Armstrong Roberts, 34, 58, 67, 75; Tom Stack, 4, 73; Sterling Studios, 76; United States Department of Agriculture, 30.

ISBN 0-89542-063-5 395

Editorial Director, James Kuse

Managing Editor, Ralph Luedtke

Production Editor/Manager, Richard Lawson

Photographic Editor, Gerald Koser

designed and edited by

David Schansberg

In those vernal seasons of the year, when the air is calm and pleasant, it were an injury and sullenness against nature not to go out and see her riches, and partake in her rejoicing.

John Milton

I pity the person who does not get at least one or two fresh impressions of the charm and sweetness of nature in the spring. Later in the season it gets to be more of an old story; but in March, when the season is early, and in April, when the season is late, there occasionally come days which awaken a new joy in the heart. Every recurring spring one experiences this fresh delight. There is nothing very tangible yet in awakening nature, but there is something in the air, some sentiment in the sunshine and in the look of things, a prophecy of life and renewal, that sends a thrill through the frame.

John Burroughs

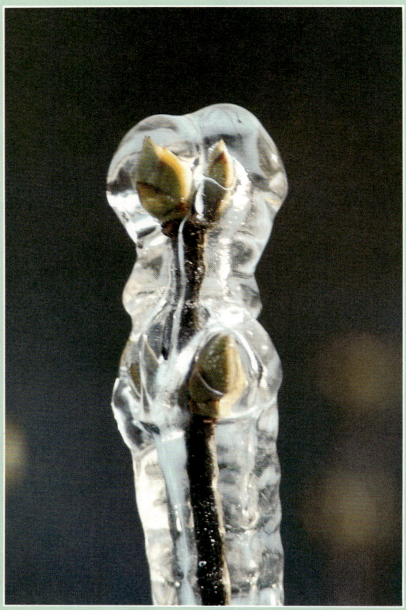

. . . morning is the time to see in perfection the woods and shrubs wearing their snowy and frosty dress. Even he who visits them half an hour after sunrise will have lost some of the most delicate and fleeting beauties

Henry David Thoreau

Winter again; the woods are powdered with snow this morning, and every twig is cased in glittering frostwork . . . but it is thawing fast, and before night they will be quite green again.

Susan Fenimore Cooper

Early spring buds encased by a March ice storm.

To anyone who has spent a winter in the north and known the depths to which the snow can reach, known the weeks when the mercury stays below zero, the first hint of spring is a major event. You must live in the north to understand it. You cannot just come up for it as you might go to Florida for the sunshine and the surf. To appreciate it, you must wait for it a long time, hope and dream about it, and go through considerable enduring.

Sigurd F. Olson

We are eager for Winter to be gone, since he, too, is fugitive and cannot keep his place. Invisible hands deface his icy statuary; his chisel has lost its cunning. The drifts, so pure and exquisite, are now earth-stained and weather-worn—the flutes and scallops, and fine, firm lines, all gone; and what was a grace and an ornament to the hills is now a disfiguration.

But he will not abdicate without a struggle. Day after day he rallies his scattered forces, and night after night pitches his white tents on the hills, and would fain regain his lost ground; but the young prince in every encounter prevails. Slowly and reluctantly the gray old hero retreats up the mountain, till finally the south rain comes in earnest, and in a night he is dead.

John Burroughs

ly morning frost creates a delicate pattern on
w seasons early plant growth.

Spring in the north begins while the land is still frozen and white. It comes with the winds and gales and drifting snows toward mid-March in a barely perceptible hint of warmth as the sun climbs high. As days lengthen there are smells of balsam and pine and warming earth on southern slopes. And if one listens, there are telltale sounds as well: the crystalline tinkling of melting ice and snow, the soft chuckling of running water in creeks and in millions of rivulets breaking free. Toward April there are new bird songs, the keening of killdeer in low places, the mating whistle of chickadees in the balsams, the mewing of seagulls along open leads of water on the lakes. And there are colors too: a rosy-purplish blush in the tops of birches, dogwood stems red against the white.

As snowbanks sink and then disappear, there are drifts of pussy willows in still frozen swamps and then, almost overnight, a brush of Nile green on aspen-covered ridges and in warm cozy nooks out of the wind the rosy hue of maples bursting into bloom. Though the forest floor is still brown and the smell of it is of mold and wetness, by mid-May it is gay with blue and white hepatica, pink anemones, and— along the flooded banks of creeks—marsh marigolds.

All life is stirring now in lakes, and ponds, and streams, and in myriad tiny pools of snow water. The earth is awake at last after the long winter's sleep, and within it is a quickening. After half a year of frozen silence, spring is a miracle of rebirth, a time of rare transcendent beauty and promise.

Sigurd F. Olson

I forgot my work and all immediate responsibilities and went out of doors. On the sunny side of the house I stood and looked and waited, expecting something to happen, but the drifts were the same and the wind out of the northwest was not different from the gales that had piled the snows for the past months. Then I became conscious of the sound of trickling water beside me—nothing more than a whisper, but the forerunner, I knew, of a million coming trickles that would take down the drifts of the entire countryside.

It was there that I got my first real whiff of spring: the smell of warming trees, pines and balsams and resins beginning to soften on the south slopes. I waited there and sniffed like a hound on the loose, winnowing through my starved nostrils the whole composite picture of coming events.

Sigurd F. Olson

The change from storm and winter serene and mild weather, from dar and sluggish hou to bright and elas ones, is a memor- able crisis which things proclaim. I seemingly instan neous at last.

Henry David T

We are slow to realize water, — the beauty and magic of it. It is interestingly strange to us forever . . .

Henry David Thoreau

On the 13th of March, after I had heard the bluebird, song sparrow, and the redwing, the ice was still nearly a foot thick. As the weather grew warmer it was not sensibly worn away by the water, nor broken up and floated off as in rivers, but, though it was completely melted for half a rod in width about the shore, the middle was merely honeycombed and saturated with water, so that you could put your foot through it when six inches thick; but by the next day evening, after a warm rain followed by fog, it would have wholly disappeared, all gone off with the fog, spirited away.

Henry David Thoreau

Every incident connected with the breaking up of the rivers and ponds and the settling of the weather is particularly interesting to us who live in a climate of so great extremes. When the warmer days come, they who dwell near the river hear the ice crack at night with a startling whoop as loud as artillery, as if its icy fetters were rent from end to end, and within a few days see it rapidly going out.

Henry David Thoreau

One attraction in coming to the woods to live was that I should have leisure and opportunity to see the spring come in. The ice in the pond at length begins to be honeycombed, and I can set my heel in it as I walk. Fogs and rains and warmer suns are gradually melting the snow; the days have grown sensibly longer; and I see how I shall get through the winter without adding to my woodpile, for large fires are no longer necessary.

7

Henry David Thoreau

The river never seems so much a thing of life as in the spring when it first slips off its icy fetters. The dead comes to life before one's very eyes. The rigid, pallid river is resurrected in a twinkling.

John Burroug

As streams thaw and begin to flow again, each drop of melting snow adds to the swelling sound of running, live water.

That dark-eyed water, especially where I see it at right angles with the direction of the sun, is it not the first sign of spring? How its darkness contrasts with the general lightness of the winter! It has more life in it than any part of the earth's surface. It is where one of the arteries of the earth is palpable, visible.

Henry David Thoreau

In the spring, after all the avalanches are down and the snow is melting fast, it is glorious to hear the streams sing out on the mountains. Every fountain swelling, countless rills hurry together to the rivers at the call of the sun,—beginning to run and sing soon after sunrise, increasing until toward sundown, then gradually failing through the cold frosty hours of the night. Thus the volume of the upper rivers, even in floodtime, is nearly doubled during the day, rising and falling as regularly as the tides of the sea.

John Muir

Live water heals memories. I look up the creek and here it
comes, the future, being borne aloft as on a winding succession of laden trays. You may wake and look from the window and
breathe the real air, and say, with satisfaction or with longing, "This
is it." But if you look up the creek, if you look up the creek in any
weather, your spirit fills, and you are saying, with an exulting rise of
the lungs, "Here it comes!"

Annie Dillard

9

Another pleasant feature of spring, which I have not mentioned, is the full streams. Riding across the country one bright day in March, I saw and felt, as if for the first time, what an addition to the satisfaction one has in the open air at this season are the clear, full watercourses. They come to the front, as it were, and lure and hold the eye. There are no weeds, or grasses, or foliage to hide them; they are full to the brim, and fuller; they catch and reflect the sunbeams, and are about the only objects of life and motion in

Soon the sound of thundering water diminishes, and is slowly replaced by the rustling sounds of young leaves along the banks.

nature. The trees stand so still, the fields are so hushed and naked, the mountains so exposed and rigid, that the eye falls upon the blue, sparkling, undulating watercourses with a peculiar satisfaction.

The little brown brooks,—how swift and full they ran! One fancied something gleeful and hilarious in them. And the large creeks,—how steadily they rolled on, trailing their ample skirts along the edges of the fields and marshes, and leaving ragged patches of water here and there! Many a gentle slope spread, as it were, a turfy apron in which reposed a little pool or lakelet. Many a stream sent little detachments across lots, the sparkling water seeming to trip lightly over the unbroken turf. Here and there an oak or an elm stood knee-deep in a clear pool, as if rising from its bath. It gives one a fresh, genial feeling to see such a bountiful supply of pure, running water. One's desires and affinities go out toward the full streams. How many a parched place they reach and lap in one's memory! How many a vision of naked pebbles and sun-baked banks they cover and blot out! They give eyes to the fields; they give dimples and laughter; they give light and motion. *Running water!* What a delightful suggestion the words always convey! One's thoughts and sympathies are set flowing by them; they unlock a fountain of pleasant fancies and associations in one's memory; the imagination is touched and refreshed.

March water is usually clean, sweet water; every brook is a trout-brook, a mountain brook; the cold and the snow have supplied the condition of a high latitude; no stagnation, no corruption, comes downstream now as on a summer freshet. Winter comes down, liquid and repentant. Indeed, it is more than water that runs then: it is frost subdued; it is spring triumphant. No obsolete watercourses now. The larger creeks seek out their abandoned beds, return to the haunts of their youth, and linger fondly there.

John Burroughs

The Brook in the Woods

Fallen logs across the stream,
A quiet spot to rest and dream,
The trickling water's little sound,
The gnarled old roots in mossy mound,
The ferns in delicate design
Pay homage to the stately pine.
The water falls into a pool.
The timid deer find it so cool.
The cedar, birch so intertwined,

Seclusion here and peace of mind.
The sparrow adds his sweet gay song.
This is the place to linger long,
Gaze up at clouds so fluffy white
And see the leaves that catch the light.
The crashing of the sea off shore
Seems such a clamor, such a roar.
This refuge, though, is still of sound,
A haven that the deer have found!

Barbara Moran

For thou, O spring! canst renovate
All that high God did first create.
Be still his arm and architect,
Rebuild the ruin, mend defect;
Chemist to vamp old worlds with new,
Coat sea and sky with heavenlier blue,
New-tint the plumage of the birds,
And slough decay from grazing herds,
Sweep ruins from the scarped mountain,
Cleanse the torrent at the fountain,
Purge alpine air by towns defiled,
Bring to fair mother fairer child,
Not less renew the heart and brain,
Scatter the sloth, wash out the stain,
Make the aged eye sun-clear,
To parting soul bring grandeur near.
Under gentle types, my spring
Masks the might of nature's king,
An energy that searches thorough
From chaos to the dawning morrow;
Into all our human plight,
The soul's pilgrimage and flight;
In city or in solitude,
Step by step, lifts bad to good,
Without halting, without rest,
Lifting better up to best;
Planting seeds of knowledge pure,
Through earth to ripen, through heaven endure.

Ralph Waldo Emerson

A cattail in bloom: one of the first signs of spring in the marshes.

This is the first really spring day, something analogous to the thawing of the ice seems to have taken place in the air. At the end of winter there is a season in which we are daily expecting spring, and finally a day when it arrives. Methinks the first obvious evidence of spring is the pushing out of the swamp willow catkins, then the pushing up of skunk cabbage spathes (and pads at the bottom of water).

Henry David Thoreau

All beginnings in nature afford us a peculiar pleasure. The early spring with its hints and dim prophecies, the first earth odors, the first robin or song sparrow, the first furrow, the first tender skies, the first rainbow, the first wild flower, the dropping bud scales, the awakening voices in the marshes—all these things touch and move us in a way that later developments in the season do not.

John Burroughs

These earliest spring days are peculiarly pleasant. We shall have no more of them for a year. I am apt to forget that we may have raw and blustering days a month hence. The combination of this delicious air, which you do not want to be warmer or softer, with the presence of ice and snow, you sitting on the bare russet portions, the south hillsides, of the earth, this is the charm of these days. It is the summer beginning to show itself like an old friend in the midst of winter. You ramble from one drier russet patch to another. These are your stages. You have the air and sun to summer, over snow and ice, and in some places even the rustling of dry leaves under your feet, as in Indian summer days.

Henry David Thoreau

How silent are the footsteps of Spring! . . . though the rest of the meadow is covered with snow a foot or more in depth, I am surprised to see the skunk cabbage, with its great spearheads open and ready to blossom. The spring advances in spite of snow and ice, and cold even.

Henry David Thoreau

pring is the inspira-
on, fall the expira-
on. Both seasons
ave their equinoxes,
oth their filmy,
azy air, their ruddy
rest tints, their cold
ins, their drenching
gs, their mystic
oons; both have the
me solar light and
armth, the same
ys of the sun; yet,
ter all, how different
e feelings which
ey inspire! One is
e morning, the other
e evening; one is
uth, the other is
e . . .

John Burroughs

Thoreau, as revealed in his journal, was for years trying to settle in his own mind what was the first thing that stirred in spring, after the severe New England winter,—in what was the first sign or pulse of returning life manifest; and he never seems to have been quite sure. He could not get his salt on the tail of this bird. He dug into the swamps, he peered into the water, he felt with benumbed hands for the radical leaves of the plants under the snow; he inspected the buds on the willows, the catkins on the alders; he went out before daylight of a March morning and remained out after dark; he watched the lichens and mosses on the rocks; he listened for the birds; he was on the alert for the first frog ("Can you be absolutely sure," he says, "that you have heard the first frog that croaked in the township?"); he stuck a pin here and he stuck a pin there, and there, and still he could not satisfy himself. Nor can any one.

John Burroughs

Nature is always new in the spring, and lucky are we if it finds us new also.

John Burroughs

All change is a miracle to contemplate; but it is a miracle which is taking place every instant.

Henry David Thoreau

Ecstasy

To hit that high sweet moment of the spring,
When sky and earth and every living thing
Seems to be part of some vast throbbing whole,
The life and breath, the body and the soul
Of vaster world beyond our mortal ken,
And greater than the dreams of common men.

Perhaps the moment that a bluebird came
Catching the early sunlight like a flame
Against the blossoms on an apple bough;
Or a young bride whispering her marriage vow,
Her blue eyes starry bright to match the gleam
Of the divine fulfillment of her dream.

Perhaps blue smoke from a low stubble fire
Held in itself the warmth of spring's desire;
A cowbell from a pasture field nearby,
A flock of sea gulls circling in the sky,
The whistle of a train that seems to hold
Adventure in a cup of purest gold.

Perhaps the moment came all unaware
Straight from the heart of springtime. It was there
Shouting from hedge and field and swaying tree,
From sun and wind and stars . . . the ecstasy
Flowed and enveloped every living thing
And all creation cried, "Behold the spring."

Edna Jaques

In the soft rose and pale gold of the declining light, this beautiful evening, I heard the first hum and preparation of awakening spring, very faint, whether in the earth or roots, or starting of insects, I know not; but it was audible, as I lean'd on a rail (I am down in my country quarters awhile,) and look'd long at the western horizon.

Walt Whitman

Maple sap is collected in tin buckets (right and drawing below) and then taken to a sugar house (above) where the sap is boiled down to make maple syrup.

Maple sugar; a wild delicacy no other sweet can match.

Before the bud swells, before the grass springs, before the plow is started, comes the sugar harvest. It is the sequel of the bitter frost; a sap-run is the sweet good-by of winter. It denotes a certain equipoise of the season; the heat of the day fully balances the frost of the night. As the days and nights get equal, the heat and cold get equal, and the sap mounts. A day that brings the bees out of the hive will bring the sap out of the maple tree. It is the fruit of the equal marriage of the sun and frost. Sugar weather is crisp weather. How the tin buckets glisten in the gray woods; how the robins laugh; how the nuthatches call; how lightly the thin blue smoke rises among the trees! The squirrels are out of their dens;

... of the features of farm life peculiar to this country, and one of the most picturesque of them all, is sugar-making in the maple woods in spring. This is the first work of the season, and to the boys is more play than work.

John Burrough[s]

Buckets of sap are carried to a large tub on a horse-drawn sled with the aid of a neck yoke. The sap is then transported to the boiling tubs in the sugar house.

the migrating waterfowls are streaming northward; the sheep and cattle look wistfully toward the bare fields; the tide of the season, in fact, is just beginning to rise.

In my sugar-making days, the sap was carried to the boiling-place in pails by the aid of a neck yoke and stored in hogsheads, and boiled or evaporated in immense kettles or caldrons set in huge stone arches; now, the hogshead goes to the trees hauled upon a sled by a team, and the sap is evaporated in broad, shallow, sheet-iron pans,—a great saving of fuel and of labor.

Many a farmer sits up all night boiling his sap, when the run has been an extra good one, and a lonely vigil he has of it amid the silent trees and besides his wild hearth. If he has a sap-house, as is now so common, he may make himself fairly comfortable; and if a companion, he may have a good time or a glorious wake.

Maple sugar in its perfection is rarely seen, perhaps never seen, in the market. When made in large quantities and indifferently, it is dark and coarse; but when made in small quantities—that is, quickly from the first run of sap and properly treated—it has a wild delicacy of flavor that no other sweet can match. What you smell in freshly cut maple wood, or taste in the blossom of the tree, is in it. It is then, indeed, the distilled essence of the tree. Made into syrup, it is white and clear as clover honey; and crystallized into sugar, it is pure as the wax. The way to attain this result is to evaporate the sap under cover in an enameled kettle; when reduced about twelve times, allow it to settle half a day or more; then clarify with milk or the white of an egg. The product is virgin syrup, or sugar worthy the table of the gods.

John Burroughs

Fresh maple sugar offered for sale today. A large amount of this sugar is still made in our neighborhood, chiefly for home consumption on the farms, where it is a matter of regular household use, many families depending on it altogether, keeping only a little white sugar for sickness; and it is said that children have grown up in this county without tasting any but maple sugar.

Some farmers have a regular "sugar bush," where none but maples are suffered to grow; and on the older farms you occasion-

sugar house, sap is carefully boiled in large vats.

Sap's Running

Sap's running in the maple trees,
   The smell of earth is in the air.
Although the wind is raw and cold
   The feel of spring is everywhere.
This morning 'ere the sun came up
   I saw a robin zooming down,
A hardy pioneer no doubt,
   Looking up housing in the town.

The maple bush is all alive,
   With light and shade and pitted snow.
Blue smoke is drifting through the trees;
   Above a hill I heard a crow
Giving a broadcast of events
   To fellow crows, who listened in
From the split rail atop the fence.

On every maple tree there hangs
   A wooden pail to catch the sap,
As drop by drop it slowly falls
   From the small nozzle of the tap.
In the pale liquid, clear as wine,
   A few small twigs and leaves have blown,
Combining with the frost and sun
   To give a flavor of their own.

A dozen children gather round
   The steaming kettles' fragrant glow,
Begging their dad to pour the sap
   Into their little pans of snow.
Earth holds no greater joy, I swear,
   No sweeter charm can heaven bring,
Than maple trees warmed by the sun
   Where sap is running in the spring.

Edna Jaques

ally pass a beautiful grove of this kind entirely clear of underwood, the trees standing on a smooth green turf. More frequently, however, a convenient spot is chosen in the woods where maples are plenty. The younger trees are not tapped, as they are injured by the process; it is only after they have reached a good size—ten or twelve inches in diameter—that they are turned to account in this way; twenty years at least must be their age, as they rarely attain to such a growth earlier; from this period they continue to yield their sap freely until they decay. It is really surprising that any tree should afford to lose so much of its natural nourishment without injury; but maples that have been tapped for fifty years, or more, seem just as luxuriant in their foliage and flowers as those that are untouched. The amount of sap yielded by different trees varies—some will give nearly three times as much as others; the fluid taken from one tree is also much sweeter and richer than that of another; there seems to be a constitutional difference between them. From two to five pounds of sugar are made from each tree, and four or five gallons of sap are required to every pound.

Susan Fenimore Cooper

... a farmer sits up all night boiling his sap, when the run has been an extra good one, and a lonely vigil he has of it amid the silent trees and beside his wild hearth.

John Burroughs

Making maple syrup is a tedious, time consuming process. A farmer often stays up all night to maintain a constant boiling temperature beneath the bubbling sap.

Man can have but one interest in nature, namely, to see himself reflected or interpreted there...

John Burroughs

Spring has returned and has begun to unfold her beautiful array; to throw herself on wild flower couches, to walk abroad on the hills and summon her songsters to do her sweet homage. This soft bewitching luxury of vernal gales and accompanying beauty overwhelms. It produces a lassitude which is full of mental enjoyment and which we would not exchange for more vigorous pleasure. Although so long as the spell endures, little or nothing is accomplished, nevertheless, I believe it operates to divert the mind of old and worn-out contemplations and bestows new freshness upon life, and leaves behind it imaginations of enchantment for the mind to mould into splendid forms and gorgeous fancies which shall long continue to fascinate, after the physical phenomena which woke them have ceased to create delight.

Ralph Waldo Emerson

Actually, spring invites participation, even though it does not need human help. Sap rises in the trees, and human beings who are not urbanized beyond redemption feel something like the urgencies of sap rise in themselves. Spring brings its own renewal after the winter of attrition. We are not exactly as the grass, but when the green comes again to the pastures and the lawns, we too are renewed. Brooks flow freely again. The squirrels are capering. There is something in the very air, out beyond the pall of smog, that seems to say anything is possible.

Hal Borland

Changing Moods

What brings this sudden restlessness
On the first warm day in spring?
It bids me take myself outside
To look at everything.
With eager fingers I must probe
The damp and fragrant earth
For signs of something waiting there,
Ready to burst forth.

My winged feet are as quick to roam
As my thoughts are bound to stray,
And duties sane and sensible
Are banished for the day.
Instead I watch the clouds pile up
Into castles mountain-high;
Watch them tumble and reshape
The foothills of the sky.

Oh, airy, fairy, lightsome day,
Your sweet sorcery
Has filled the throat of every bird
With singing ecstasy.
Responding to your changing moods,
Completely under your spell,
I stand bemused, a prisoner
Where only fancies dwell.

Mary A. Selden

April is that part of the season that never cloys upon the palate. It does not surfeit one with good things, but provokes and stimulates the curiosity. One is on the alert, there are hints and suggestions on every hand. Something has just passed, or stirred, or called, or breathed, in the open air or in the ground about, that we would fain know more of. May is sweet, but April is pungent. There is frost enough in it to make it sharp, and heat enough in it to make it quick.

John Burroughs

Then the plants also are in flood; the hidden sap singing into leaf and flower, responding as faithfully to the call of the sun as the streams from the snow, gathering along the outspread roots like rills in their channels on the mountains, rushing up the stems of herb and tree, swirling in their myriad cells like streams in potholes, spreading along the branches and breaking into foamy bloom, while fragrance, like a finer music, rises and flows with the winds.

About the same may be said of the spring gladness of blood when the red streams surge and sing in accord with the swelling plants and rivers, inclining animals and everybody to travel in hurrahing crowds like floods, whole exhilarating melody in color and fragrance, form and motion, flows to the heart through all the quickening senses.

John Muir

When the Green Gits Back in the Trees

In Spring, when the green gits back in the trees,
   And the sun comes out and stays,
And yer boots pulls on with a good tight squeeze,
   And you think of yer barefoot days;
When you ort to work and you want to not,
   And you and yer wife agrees
It's time to spade up the garden lot,
   When the green gits back in the trees—
      Well! Work is the least o' my idees
      When the green, you know, gits back in the trees!

When the whole tail feathers o' wintertime
   Is all pulled out and gone!
And the sap, it thaws and begins to climb,
   And the swet it starts out on
A feller's forred, a-gittin' down
   At the old spring on his knees—
I kindo' like jest a-loafin' roun'
   When the green gits back in the trees—
      Jest a-potterin' roun' as I durn please,
      When the green, you know, gits back in the trees!

When the green gits back in the trees, and bees
   Is a-buzzin' aroun' ag'in,
In that kind of a lazy go-as-you-please
   Old gait they bum roun' in;
When the groun's all bald where the hayrick stood,
   And the crick's riz, and the breeze
Coaxes the bloom in the old dogwood,
   And the green gits back in the trees,—
      I like, as I say, in sich scenes as these,
      The time when the green gits back in the trees!

James Whitcomb Riley

23

I have thought that a good test of civilization, perhaps one of the best, is country life. Where country life is safe and enjoyable, where many of the conveniences and appliances of the town are joined to the large freedom and large benefits of the country, a high state of civilization prevails.

John Burroughs

But the farmer has the most sane and natural occupation, and ought to find life sweeter, if less highly seasoned, than any other. He alone, strictly speaking, has a home. How can a man take root and thrive without land? He writes his history upon his field. How many ties, how many resources, he has,—his friendships with his cattle, his team, his dog, his trees, the satisfaction in his growing crops, in his improved fields; his intimacy with nature, with bird and beast, and with the quickening elemental forces; his cooperations with the cloud, the sun, the seasons, heat, wind, rain, frost! Nothing will take the various social distempers which the city and artificial life breed out of a man like farming, like direct and loving contact with the soil. It draws out the poison. It humbles him, teaches him patience and reverence, and restores the proper tone to his system.

Cling to the farm, make much of it, put yourself into it, bestow your heart and your brain upon it, so that it shall savor of you and radiate your virtue after your day's work is done!

John Burroughs

The glory of the farmer is that it is his to construct and to create. Let others borrow and imitate, travel and exchange, and make fortunes by speed and dexterity in selling something which they never made. All rests at last upon his primitive activity. He stands close to nature; obtains from the earth, bread; the food which was not, he has caused to be. And this necessity and duty give the farm its dignity. All men feel this to be their natural employment.

Ralph Waldo Emerson

Blessed is he whose youth was passed upon the farm, and if it was a dairy farm his memories will be all the more fragrant. The driving of the cows to and from the pasture, every day and every season for years,—how much of summer and of nature he got into him on these journeys! What rambles and excursions did this errand furnish the excuse for! The birds and birds' nests, the berries, the squirrels, the woodchucks, the beech woods with their treasures into which the cows loved so to wander and to browse, the fragrant wintergreens and a hundred nameless adventures, all strung upon that brief journey of half a mile to and from the remote pastures.

John Burroughs

There is something to me peculiarly interesting in stone walls—a kind of rude human expression to them, suggesting the face of the old farmer himself. They decay not, yet they grow old and decrepit; little by little they lose their precision and firmness, they stagger, then fall. In a still, early spring morning or April twilight one often hears a rattle of stones in a distant field; some bit of old wall is falling.

John Burroughs

New England Stone Walls

Old stone walls, gray-mossed, and lone,
Remnant marks of labor's will,
In your lengths of fallen stone
Stretched on meadowland and hill,
You tell silently of days
When each stone on you was laid
Toilsomely, in many ways,
Till in settled clinch it stayed.

Though your first straight lines are bent,
And your topstones swept away,
Though your sagging sides are rent
Where foundations sink in clay,
Still around you firmly cling
Spirit-blooms of pioneers,
Ever freshly blossoming,
Through the dust of passing years.

Stephen Wright

The fields and woods and waters about one are a book from which he may draw exhaustless entertainment, if he will. One must not only learn the writing, he must translate the language, the signs, and the hieroglyphics. It is a very quaint and elliptical writing, and much must be supplied by the wit of the translator.

John Burroughs

An Invitation to the Country

Already, close by our summer dwelling,
   The Easter sparrow repeats her song;
A merry warbler, she chides the blossoms,
   The idle blossoms that sleep so long.

The bluebird chants, from the elm's long branches,
   A hymn to welcome the budding year.
The south wind wanders from field to forest,
   And softly whispers, "The Spring is here."

Come, daughter mine, from the gloomy city,
   Before those lays from the elm have ceased;
The violet breathes by our door, as sweetly
   As in the air of her native East.

Though many a flower in the wood is waking,
   The daffodil is our doorside queen;
She pushes upward the sward already,
   To spot with sunshine the early green.

No lays so joyous as these are warbled
   From wiry prison in maiden's bower;
No pampered bloom of the greenhouse chamber
   Has half the charm of the lawn's first flower.

Yet these sweet sounds of the early season,
   And these fair sights of its sunny days,
Are only sweet when we fondly listen,
   And only fair when we fondly gaze.

There is no glory in star or blossom
   Till looked upon by a loving eye;
There is no fragrance in April breezes
   Till breathed with joy as they wander by.

Come, Julia dear, for the sprouting willows,
   The opening flowers, and the gleaming brooks,
And hollows, green in the sun, are waiting
   Their dower of beauty from thy glad looks.

William Cullen Bryant

Still, the essential charm of the farm remains and always will remain: the care of crops, and of cattle, and of orchards, bees, and fowl; the clearing and improving of the ground; the building of barns and houses; the direct contact with the soil and with the elements; the watching of the clouds and of the weather; the privacies with nature, with bird, beast, and plant; and the close acquaintance with the heart and virtue of the world. The farmer should be the true naturalist; the book in which it is all written is open before him night and day, and how sweet and wholesome all his knowledge is!

John Burroughs

Spring Plowing

He walks the furrow's narrow way,
And measures off with sweet content
The land that glows before his eyes
With warm and pulsing wonderment;
For spring now flaunts its apple green
On meadowland and leafing boughs,
And delights the very heart and soul
Of one who guides the moving plow.

Above the horses' plodding hoofs,
Sweeps the shrill, transcendent call
Of a meadowlark that finds delight
In trilling forth its song to all;
And as the plowshare cuts its way
Through the warm and fragrant earth,
The farmer feels a joy and closeness
With the season springing into birth.

Enlivened by the morning air,
The woodsy scent from yonder grove,
He carefully turns his sturdy plow
And treads the furrow of another row;
While April's young and stirring breeze
Wafts gently past his cheek,
And ripples through the snowy crown
Of dogwood trees down by the creek.

About him lies his wealth and joy,
The fertile sod beneath his feet,
The beauty of the field and sky,
The glow of spring, fragrant and sweet.
And he walks the furrow's way
Content, from all the world apart,
With the meadowlark's sweet lilting call
Still echoing within his heart!

Joy Belle Burgess

Faith Unforgotten

Tractors now, where once a team
Pulled the walking plow's curved beam;
Giant power where the strain
Of tired muscles reaped the grain.

Motors roaring down the field
Wrest from earth an ancient yield,
Once the fruit of sweat and toil
Far more intimate with soil.

Tractors now, slow muscles then,
But the hearts of farming men
And their women cherish still
Kinship with the soil they till,
Seeing past the bright machine
To God's gift of growing green!

S. Omar Barker

It is at that period, usually late in April, when we behold the first quickening of the earth. The waters have subsided, the roads have become dry, the sunshine has grown strong and its warmth has penetrated the sod; there is a stir of preparation about the farm and all through the country. One does not care to see things very closely; his interest in nature is not special but general. The earth is coming to life again. All the genial and more fertile places in the landscape are brought out; the earth is quickened in spots and streaks; you can see at a glance where man and nature have dealt the most kindly with it. The warm, moist places, the places that have had the wash of some building or of the road, or have been subjected to some special mellowing influence, how quickly the turf awakens there and shows the tender green! See the old barn on the meadow slope; the green seems to have oozed out from it, and to have flowed slowly down the hill; at a little distance it is lost in the sere stubble. One can see where every spring lies buried about the fields; its influence is felt at the surface, and the turf is early quickened there. Where the cattle have loved to lie and ruminate in the warm summer twilight, there the April sunshine loves to linger too, till the sod thrills to new life. . . .

The full charm of this April landscape is not brought out till the afternoon. It seems to need the slanting rays of the evening sun to give it the right mellowness and tenderness, or the right perspective. It is, perhaps, a little too bald in the strong, white light of the earlier part of the day; but when the faint, four-o'clock shadows begin to come out, and we look through the green vistas, and along the farm lanes toward the west, or out across long stretches of fields above which spring seems fairly hovering, just ready to alight, and note the teams slowly plowing, the brightened mould-board gleaming in the sun now and then—it is at such times we feel its fresh, delicate attraction the most. There is no foliage on the trees yet; only here and there the red bloom of the soft maple, illuminated by the declining sun, shows vividly against the tender green of a slope beyond, or a willow, like a thin veil, stands out against a leafless wood. Here and there a little meadow watercourse is golden with marsh marigolds, or some fence border, or rocky streak of neglected pasture land, is thickly starred with the white flowers of the bloodroot. The eye can devour a succession of landscapes at such a time; there is nothing that sates or entirely fills it, but every spring token stimulates it and makes it more on the alert.

John Burroughs

The brown soil here, (just between winter-close and opening spring and vegetation)—the rain shower at night, and the fresh smell next morning—the red worms wriggling out of the ground—the dead leaves, the incipient grass, and the latent life underneath—the effort to start something—already in shelter'd spots some little flowers—the distant emerald show of winter wheat and the rye fields—the yet naked trees, with clear interstices, giving prospects hidden in summer—the tough fallow and the plow team, and the stout boy whistling to his horses for encouragement—and there the dark fat earth in long slanting stripes upturned.

Walt Whitman

One seems to get nearer to nature in the early spring days: all screens are removed, the earth everywhere speaks directly to you; she is not hidden by verdure and foliage; there is a peculiar delight in walking over the brown turf of the fields that one cannot feel later on. How welcome the smell of it, warmed by the sun; the first breath of the reviving earth.

John Burroughs

Love of the Land

A deep urge holds a man close to his land;
It springs from primal source not understood.
It is not meant for him to understand
The potent forces coursing through his blood.

The force will stretch dimensions of the mind,
Give added strength to body, soul, and heart.
A farming man can never know or find
A joy when verdant fields are far apart.

He builds his homestead, stone on painful stone.
He guides a plow through fields unharvested.
A man must live and work on land his own,
Or else his soul and mind and heart are dead.

And should he leave them, he will soon return.
His roots are planted deep in mother earth.
The soil is his life. The man will learn
Away from it, there is no life or mirth.

Roy Z. Kemp

The more earth-
worms in the soil
the more resistant it
is likely to be to the
erosion of spring.

Edwin Way Teale

e invaluable earthworm and its durable castings.

In spring when the frost has left the soil, the earthworm begins its
most active period. As the first rains of late March and April flood
their winter burrows, earthworms tunnel to the surface to escape
drowning. They slither through tender young blades of grass or
become stranded on wet pavements, vulnerable to the voracious
appetites of returning birds or awakening mammals and reptiles.
They also fall prey to eager fishermen who hope to entice trout with
hooks baited with the plump, squirming creatures. The earthworm's function, however, is more important to nature and man
than a niche in the food chain or a popular bait.

The earthworm's efficient burrowing activities are an invaluable
contribution to plant growth. This constant movement of dirt
increases the porosity of soils, thus allowing air and water to reach
even the deepest roots of plants. At the same time, earthworms
enrich the soil by transporting dead plant material into deeper soil
layers where it decays faster, providing nutrients for the plants.

While the earthworms burrow, they swallow particles of soil,
digesting organic material and passing the inorganic material
through the digestive tract. These inorganic castings are deposited
on the surface. As these castings are twice as hard as the surround-
ing soil and twice as resistant to falling raindrops, they help prevent
erosion of the land.

There can be four million earthworms in just one acre of land,
and each earthworm ingests and discards its own weight in food
and soil every day. This means that each year as much as thirty tons
of new earth is brought to the surface by these remarkable farmers.

have always believed that fishing for brook trout is a spiritual thing and that those who engage in it sooner or later are touched with its magic. All trout fishermen, even the most sophisticated of the dry-fly purists, are boys at heart, with a boy's wonder and joy in a stream, the feel of it, the sounds, and the sense of being a part of its life and movement.

Sigurd F. Olson

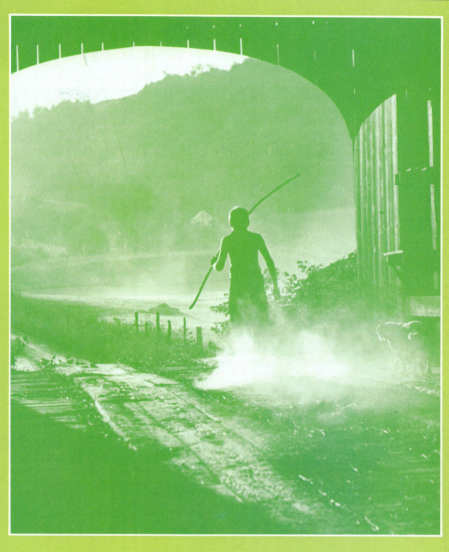

Trout streams coursed through every valley my boyhood knew. I crossed them, and was often lured and detained by them, on my way to and from school. We bathed in them during the long summer noons, and felt for the trout under their banks. A holiday was a holiday indeed that brought permission to go fishing over on Rose's Brook, or up Hardscrabble, or in Meeker's Hollow; all-day trips, from morning till night, through meadows and pastures and beechen woods, wherever the shy, limpid stream led. Alert and wide-eyed, one picked his way along, startled now and then by the sudden bursting-up of the partridge, or by the whistling wings of the "dropping snipe," pressing through the brush and the briers, or finding an easy passage over the trunk of a prostrate tree, carefully letting his hook down through some tangle into a still pool, or standing in some high, sombre avenue and watching his line float in and out amid the moss-covered boulders.

John Burroughs

Spring appears, and we are once more children, we commence again our course with the new year.

Henry David Thoreau

A Boy in Spring

A boy in spring is a happy boy
With his fishing rod and bait,
His worn-out shoes and his old slouch hat
And he's off for a special date.
Down the road and through the fence
You can hear his happy song,
His heart overflowing with springtime joys
As he joins the merry throng.

A boy in spring is a lucky boy
When the sky is clear and blue,
When school is out and it's time for play
With his daily chores all through;
Over the hills to the shaded nook
By the side of the little stream,
He and his dog will be sitting there
Aglow in a boyhood dream.

A boy in spring is a joy complete
And his laughter will thrill your heart,
Of all the precious and lovely things
He's such a great big part.
You'll hear his whistle and boyish shout,
You'll join in his happy ways . . .
A boy in spring is life's greatest joy
For he blesses springtime days.

Garnet Ann Schultz

The world the boy lives in is separate and distinct from the world the man lives in. It is a world inhabited only by boys. No events are important or of any moment save those affecting boys. How they ignore the presence of their elders on the street, shouting out their invitations, their appointments, their pass-words from our midst, as from the veriest solitude! They have peculiar calls, whistles, signals, by which they communicate with each other at long distances, like birds or wild creatures. And there is as genuine a wildness about these notes and calls as about those of a fox or coon.

34

John Burroughs

The Barefoot Boy

Blessings on thee, little man,
Barefoot boy, with cheek of tan!
With thy turned-up pantaloons
And thy merry whistled tunes;
With thy red lips redder still
Kissed by strawberries on the hill;
With the sunshine on thy face,
Through thy torn brim's jaunty grace—
From my heart I give thee joy;
I was once a barefoot boy.
Prince thou art—the grown-up man,
Only is republican.
Let the million-dollared ride!
Barefoot, trudging at his side,
Thou hast more than he can buy,
In the reach of ear and eye:
Outward sunshine, inward joy,
Blessings on the barefoot boy.

O for boyhood's painless play,
Sleep that wakes in laughing day,
Health that mocks the doctor's rules,
Knowledge never learned of schools:
Of the wild bees' morning chase,
Of the wild flower's time and place,
Flight of fowl and habitude
Of the tenants of the wood;
How the tortoise bears his shell,
How the woodchuck digs his cell,
And the ground-mole digs his well;
How the robin feeds her young,
How the oriole's nest is hung
Where the whitest lilies blow,
Where the freshest berries grow,
Where the ground nut trails its vine,
Where the wood-grape's clusters shine;
Of the black wasp's cunning way,
Mason of his walls of clay,
And the architectural plans
Of gray hornet artisans!
For, eschewing books and tasks,
Nature answers all he asks;
Hand-in-hand with her he walks,
Face to face with her he talks,
Part and parcel of her joy,
Blessings on the barefoot boy.

O for boyhood's time of June,
Crowding years in one brief moon,
When all things I heard or saw,
Me, their master, waited for!
I was rich in flowers and trees,
Humming birds and honey bees;

For my sport the squirrel played,
Plied the snouted mole his spade,
For my taste the blackberry cone
Purpled over hedge and stone;
Laughed the brook for my delight,
Through the day and through the night;
Whispering at the garden wall,
Talked with me from fall to fall;
Mine the sand-rimmed pickerel pond,
Mine the walnut slopes beyond,
Mine, on bending orchard trees,
Apples of Hesperides!
Still, as my horizon grew,
Larger grew my riches too,
All the world I saw or knew
Seemed a complex Chinese toy,
Fashioned for a barefoot boy!

O for festal dainties spread,
Like my bowl of milk and bread,
Pewter spoon and bowl of wood,
On the door stone, gray and rude!
O'er me like a regal tent,
Cloudy, ribbed, the sunset bent,
Purple-curtained, fringed with gold,
Looped in many a wind-swung fold;
While for music came the play
Of the pied frogs' orchestra;
And, to light the noisy choir,
Lit the fly his lamp of fire.
I was monarch; pomp and joy
Waited on the barefoot boy!

Cheerily, then, my little man!
Live and laugh as boyhood can;
Though the flinty slopes be hard,
Stubble-speared the new-mown sward,
Every morn shall lead thee through
Fresh baptisms of the dew;
Every evening from thy feet
Shall the cool wind kiss the heat.
All too soon these feet must hide
In the prison cells of pride,
Lose the freedom of the sod,
Like a colt's for work be shod,
Made to tread the mills of toil,
Up and down in ceaseless moil,
Happy if their track be found
Never on forbidden ground;
Happy if they sink not in
Quick and treacherous sands of sin.
Ah! that thou couldst know thy joy,
Ere it passes, barefoot boy!

John Greenleaf Whittier

Days sped by in an agony of fulfillment, yet with the knowledge that there was so much unknown and being left undone. The sheer joy of life coursed through young veins, and one could run across the prairie, splashing through shallow water and leaping small streams like any other wild creature, with head thrown back and a laughter carried by the spring wind.

Ernest Thompson Seton

Child in Spring

On greening slopes she stands in breathless wonder,
A bird of blue in flash of beauty sees,
Nor understands the sudden inner thunder
Of her heart upon beholding these:
A tulip like a miniature gold cup,
Uncurling fronds like fairy fiddleheads,
Here daffodils in ruffled hats spring up
To dance in all the drab brown flower beds.
Moments spun of rapture, silver joy
Is caught within the singing of her heart,
For childhood's spring is gold without alloy,
Of all the earth's bright newness, she is part.
A child with wonder in her heart and eyes,
A marvel is each lovely growing thing,
She's filled with such a singing, glad surprise . . .
Oh, she herself is lovely as the spring.

Ruth B. Field

There was a child
went forth every day,
And the first object
that he looked upon,
that object he became,
And that object
became part of him
for the day
or a certain part of the day
or for many years
or stretching cycles of years.

Walt Whitman

...whenever I looked
out on the pond... I
saw it throwing off its
nightly clothing of
mist, and here and
there, by degrees, its
soft ripples or its
smooth reflecting sur-
face was revealed,
while the mists, like
ghosts, were stealth-
ily withdrawing in
every direction into
the woods...

Henry David Thoreau

*erie mist dances across the surface of a pond on
rly spring morning.

A cold fog. These mornings those who walk in grass are thoroughly wetted above midleg. All the earth is dripping wet. I am surprised to feel how warm the water is, by contrast with the cold, foggy air. The frogs seem glad to bury themselves in it. The dewy cobwebs are very thick this morning, little napkins of the fairies spread on the grass.

Henry David Thoreau

Mist

Low-anchored cloud,
Newfoundland air,
Fountainhead and source of rivers,
Dewcloth, dream drapery,
And napkin spread by fays;
Drifting meadow of the air,
Where bloom the daisied banks and violets.
And in whose fenny labyrinth
The bittern booms and heron wades;
Spirit of lakes and seas and rivers,
Bear only perfumes and the scent
Of healing herbs to just men's fields!

Henry David Thoreau

I perceive the spring in the softened air, apparently in consequence of the very warm sun falling on the earth, four-fifths covered with snow and ice, there is an almost invisible vapor held in suspension. Looking through this transparent vapor, all surfaces, not osiers and open water alone, look more vivid. The hardness of winter is relaxed.

Henry David Thoreau

I t was late May, before dawn and the first calling of the birds. The lake was breathing softly as in sleep; rising and falling it seemed to me, absorbing like a great sponge all the last sounds of spring: the tiny trickles, the tinklings and whisperings from still-thawing banks of hidden snow and ice. No wind rustled the leaves; there was no lapping of water against the shore, no sound of any kind. But I listened just the same, straining with all my faculties toward something—I knew not what—trying to catch the meanings that were in that moment before the lifting of the dark.

Standing there alone, I felt alive, more aware and receptive than ever before. A shout or a movement would have destroyed the spell. This was a time for silence, for being in pace with ancient rhythms and timelessness, the breathing of the lake, the slow growth of living things. Here the cosmos could be felt and the true meaning of attunement.

Sigurd F. Olson

At length the sun's rays have attained the right angle, and warm winds blow up mist and rain and melt the snowbanks, and the sun dispersing the mist smiles on a checkered landscape of russet and white smoking with incense.

Henry David Thoreau

Early morning in the wilderness is the time for smells. Before senses have become contaminated with common orders, while they are still aware and receptive, is the time to go hunting. Winnow the morning air before it is adulterated with the winds and the full blaze of sunlight, and, no matter where you happen to be, you will find something worth remembering.

Sigurd F. Olson

This was a typical March day, clear, dry, hard, and windy, the river rumpled and crumpled, the sky intense, distant objects strangely near; a day full of strong light, unusual; an extraordinary lightness and clearness all around the horizon, as if there were a diurnal aurora streaming up and burning through the sunlight; smoke from the first spring fires rising up in various directions; a day that winnowed the air, and left no film in the sky.

John Burroughs

I have penetrated to those meadows on the morning of many a first spring day, jumping from hummock to hummock, from willow root to willow root, when the wild river valley and the woods were bathed in so pure and bright a light as would have waked the dead, if they had been slumbering in their graves, as some suppose. There needs no stronger proof of immortality. All things must live in such a light.

Henry David Thoreau   41

Wet-Weather Talk

It hain't no use to grumble and complane;
    It's jest as cheap and easy to rejoice.—
When God sorts out the weather and sends rain,
    W'y, rain's my choice.

Men ginerly, to all intents—
    Although they're apt to grumble some—
Puts most theyr trust in Providence,
    And takes things as they come—
        This is, the commonality
        Of men that's lived as long as me
        Has watched the world enough to learn
        They're not the boss of this concern.

With some, of course, it's different—
    I've saw young men that knowed it all,
And didn't like the way things went
    On this terrestchul ball;—
        But all the same, the rain, some way,
        Rained jest as hard on picnic day;
        Er, when they railly wanted it,
        It mayby wouldn't rain a bit!

In this existence, dry and wet
    Will overtake the best of men—
Some little skift o'clouds'll shet
    The sun off now and then.—
        And mayby, whilse you're wundern who
        You've fool-like lent your umbrell' to,
        And want it—out'll pop the sun,
        And you'll be glad you hain't got none!

It aggervates the farmers, too—
    They's too much wet, or too much sun,
Er work, er waitin' round to do
    Before the plowin''s done:
        And mayby, like as not, the wheat,
        Jest as it's lookin' hard to beat,
        Will ketch the storm—and jest about
        The time the corn's a-jintin' out.

These-here cy-clones a-foolin' round—
    And back'ard crops!—and wind and rain!—
And yit the corn that's wallerd down
    May elbow up again!—
        They hain't no sense, as I can see,
        Fer mortuls, sich as us, to be
        A-faultin' Natchur's wise intents,
        And lockin' horns with Providence!

It hain't no use to grumble and complane;
    It's jest as cheap and easy to rejoice.—
When God sorts out the weather and sends rain,
    W'y, rain's my choice.

James Whitcomb Riley

I hear late tonight the unspeakable rain, mingled with rattling snow against the windows, preparing the ground for spring.

Henry David Thoreau

April

A high wind, a wild wind, a wet wind blowing,
April running down the hill with flowers in her hair.
The wayside pools are fluted gray, they will not be showing
How the young girl, April, looks, when she passes there.

In the tallest maples there are red buds dripping,
And blackbirds, flocks of them, shrill with their cries,
A whir of them, a stir of them, a-wheeling and dipping . . .
Who has not seen blackbirds under April skies?

Who has not loved blowing leaves in the April weather,
Little tender, growing leaves, shimmering with light?
Who is there who has not loved a flock of birds together,
Tilting on a topmost bough, resting from a flight?

A high wind, a wild wind, a wet wind blowing . . .
Is there one who does not feel his heart lift high,
With April running down the hill, and maple buds showing,
And the year's first blackbirds, shrill against the sky?

Grace Noll Crowell

How much good the rain would do, how fresh the water in every stream, how flowers would pop with the sun, the linnaea, the anemones, the dogwood and everything else along the trails! The ferns on the rocks would begin to grow again, and the silvery caribou moss would be soft and resilient with just a tinge of green. The dry and brittle lichens along the cliffs would turn from black to velvet green. Mushrooms and toadstools would suddenly emerge from every dead log, and the dusty humus would bring forth growths that had been waiting for this very hour, for no rain had fallen in a month.

The coming of the rain soothed a longing within me for moisture and lushness after the long-continued spring drought. As I lay there, I too seemed to expand and grow, become part of the lushness and the rain itself and of all the thirsty life about me.

Sigurd F. Olson

The Norway maples along the way are dropping the small keys with unmaturing seeds. They were stripped off by rains in the night. The keys with growing seeds are still expanding on the branches overhead. In nothing is the prodigal bounty of nature more apparent than in the inexhaustible surplus of flowers and seeds.

Edwin Way Tea

Roots and Leaves Themselves Alone

Roots and leaves themselves alone are these;
Scents brought to men and women from the wild woods, and from the pondside,
Breast-sorrel and pinks of love—fingers that wind around tighter than vines,
Gushes from the throats of birds hid in the foliage of trees, as the sun is risen;
Breezes of land and love—breezes set from living shores out to you on the living sea—to you, O sailors!
Frost-mellow'd berries, and third-month twigs, offer'd fresh to young persons wandering out in the fields when the winter breaks up,
Love-buds, put before you and within you, whoever you are,
Buds to be unfolded on the old terms;
If you bring the warmth of the sun to them, they will open, and bring form, color, perfume, to you;
If you become the aliment and the wet, they will become flowers, fruits, tall branches and trees.

Walt Whitman

The bud scales strew the ground in spring as the leaves do in the fall, though they are so small that we hardly notice them. All growth, all development, is a casting off, a leaving of something behind. First the bud scales drop, then the flower drops, then the fruit drops, then the leaf drops. The first two are preparatory and stand for spring; the last two are the crown and stand for autumn.

John Burroughs

The bud scales begin to drop in April, and by May Day the scales have fallen from the eyes of every branch in the forest. In most cases the bud has an inner wrapping that does not fall so soon. In the hickory this inner wrapping is like a great livid membrane, an inch or more in length, thick, fleshy, and shining. It clasps the tender leaves about as if both protecting and nursing them. As the leaves develop, these membranous wrappings curl back, and finally wither and fall. In the plane-tree, or sycamore, this inner wrapping of the bud is a little pelisse of soft yellow or tawny fur. When it is cast off, it is the size of one's thumb nail, and suggests the delicate skin of some golden-haired mole. The young sycamore balls lay aside their fur wrappings early in May. The flower tassels of the European maple, too, come packed in a slightly furry covering. The long and fleshy inner scales that enfold the flowers and leaves are of a clear olive green, thinly covered with silken hairs like the young of some animals. Our sugar maple is less striking and beautiful in the bud, but the flowers are more graceful and fringe-like.

John Burroughs

Nature never makes haste; her systems revolve at an even pace. The bud swells imperceptibly, without hurry or confusion, as though the short spring days were an eternity.

Henry David Thoreau

Within a little more than a fortnight the woods, from bare twigs, have become a sea of verdure, and young shoots have contended with one another in the race. The leaves are unfurled all over the country.

Shade is produced, and the birds are concealed and their economies go forward uninterruptedly, and a covert is afforded to animals generally. But thousands of worms and insects are preying on the leaves while they are young and tender. Myriads of little parasols are suddenly spread all the country over, to shield the earth and the roots of the trees from the parching heat, and they begin to flutter and rustle in the breeze.

Henry David Thoreau

Birch Beauty

The birch tree flaunts its beauty
At the dull unawakened trees;
Its peeling bark calling attention
As it flutters in the breeze;
Dainty pinks and lavenders mellow,
Splattered 'tween hues of tender yellow,
Ruffling out to reveal the ivory tree,
Posing erect for the early spring woods to see.

Frances E. Heldt

Weeping Willow Tree

The weeping willow is a charming tree,
With plume-like branches drooping all around,
Like lacy curtains reaching to the ground.
Beneath this cool retreat you may find peace
And rest awhile, and feel a real release
From petty cares. And you may dream at will
Amid such loveliness, where all is still
Except the whispering leaves and soft bird calls
Heard as the passing breeze rises and falls;
Sunlight makes golden patterns on the grass,
While overhead fantastic cloud shapes pass;
Green branches brush you gently as they sway
Serenely back and forth in childish play,
Till you are borne on lightest wings of sleep
Beneath the graceful weeping willow tree.

Annette May Jones

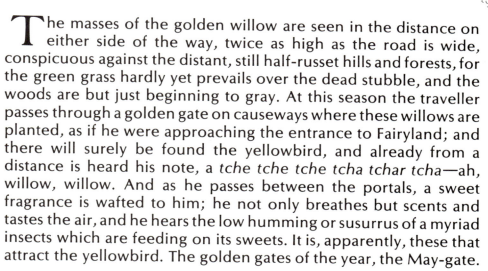

The masses of the golden willow are seen in the distance on either side of the way, twice as high as the road is wide, conspicuous against the distant, still half-russet hills and forests, for the green grass hardly yet prevails over the dead stubble, and the woods are but just beginning to gray. At this season the traveller passes through a golden gate on causeways where these willows are planted, as if he were approaching the entrance to Fairyland; and there will surely be found the yellowbird, and already from a distance is heard his note, a *tche tche tche tcha tchar tcha*—ah, willow, willow. And as he passes between the portals, a sweet fragrance is wafted to him; he not only breathes but scents and tastes the air, and he hears the low humming or susurrus of a myriad insects which are feeding on its sweets. It is, apparently, these that attract the yellowbird. The golden gates of the year, the May-gate.

Henry David Thoreau

Beside the road, at the edge of the salt meadows, someone has dumped the limbs and trunk of a willow tree. The logs have been lying there a good part of the winter. Today, as I walked past, I noticed that sprouts have pushed out all along the length of one of the logs. I stooped to count them. The seven-foot log was about eight inches in diameter at one end and about four at the other. One hundred and fifty-six sprouts had pushed out from the wet wood of this discarded log. The sight recalled the experience of a gentleman of this vicinity who placed rustic chairs about his yard. He left them out all winter. In the spring, he discovered that every chair had taken root. The rustic wood was willow.

Edwin Way Teale

The aspens are in leaf, and look beau fully on the hillside their tremulous foli age being among th very earliest to pla in the spring breeze as their downy seed are the first of the year to fly abroad; .

Susan Fenimore Co

Standing in the meadow near the early aspen at the island, I hear the first fluttering of leaves, a peculiar sound at first unaccountable to me. The breeze causes the now fully expanded aspen leaves to rustle with a pattering sound, striking one another. It is much like a gentle surge breaking on a shore, or the rippling of waves. This is the first softer music which the wind draws from the forest, the woods generally being comparatively bare and just bursting into leaf. It was delicious to behold that dark mass and hear that soft rippling sound.

Henry David Thoreau

The flowering dogwood is brighter still in these brooding days, for every branch of its broad head is then a brilliant crimson flame. In the spring, when the streams are in flood, it is the whitest of trees, white as a snow bank with its magnificent flowers four to eight inches in width, making a wonderful show, and drawing swarms of moths and butterflies.

John Muir

son blossoms of the flowering dogwood.

Apple Blossoms

I stood in the midst of an orchard
On a bright sunny morning in May,
The trees were loaded with blossoms,
Each one like a huge bouquet.

I lifted my arms to the heavens
And breathed in the sweetest perfume,
While gazing in admiration,
Adoring each precious bloom.

If only they'd stay here forever,
I would stand and admire them each day.
However, there must be fruition,
Perhaps it is better this way.

The lovely red apples at fall time
Will vie with the blossoms gay,
That smell so fragrant in springtime
Bedecked in their fine array.

J. Marie Phillips

The apple blossoms are charmingly fragrant now; they have certainly the most delightful perfume all our northern fruit trees.

Susan Fenimore Coo

As the season progresses, the sun grows continually warmer causing apple blossoms to burst forth from their buds.

50

Mountain bumblebees, queens searching for nest sites, 5,000 feet above sea level, droned past us to alight and investigate holes in the dense green carpet of moss. And once, stealing silently along the trail, we came within a few yards of blue-headed vireo singing in a dead birch. It slid away down the slope from tree to tree, bursting into its sweet, slurring song at each new perch. Everywhere around us we saw signs of a mountain spring.

Edwin Way Teale

The season was advancing swiftest along the valleys; its high-water mark was lifting little by little up the mountainsides. Like floods of water, the floods of spring follow a lowland course. They race ahead down the long valleys, climb slowly, as though struggling with gravity, up the slopes. In the mountains the streams, the highways and the railroads go through the gaps together. And with them goes spring.

Edwin Way Teale

Each hundred feet of elevation, theoretically, represents one day's advance of spring. In mountain country, however, the wheel of the seasons speeds up. Spring advances faster the higher it goes.

Edwin Way Teale

51

Considering the lilies as you go up the mountains, the first you come to is L. Pardalinum, with large orange-yellow, purple-spotted flowers big enough for babies' bonnets. It is seldom found higher than thirty-five hundred feet above the sea, grows in magnificent groups of fifty to a hundred or more, in romantic waterfall dells in the pine woods shaded by overarching maple and willow, alder and dogwood, with bushes in front of the embowering trees for a border, and ferns and sedges in front of the bushes; while the bed of black humus in which the bulbs are set is carpeted with mosses and liverworts. These richly furnished lily gardens are the pride of the falls on the lower tributaries of the Tuolumne and Merced rivers, falls not like those of Yosemite valleys,—coming from the sky with rock-shaking thunder tones,—but small, with low, kind voices cheerily singing in calm leafy bowers, self-contained, keeping their snowy skirts well about them, yet furnishing plenty of spray for the lilies.

John Muir

Our lives touched it at this one point, at this one time in spring when its magical beauty was unrivaled. Along the path to the falls we hardly advanced a foot without pausing to delight in some new wildflower. White violets blooming among hepaticas; the umbrella leaves of the mandrake sheltering the forming May apples; the massed plants of the false Solomon's seal crowding together on a rocky ledge; the white Dutchman's-breeches and the red columbine—the Jack-in-trousers—these, each in turn, attracted our attention. We bent close to see foam flowers that enveloped their upright stems in little clouds of white. The tip of each tiny floret seemed dipped in wax of a delicate apricot hue.

Up the slopes the striped flowers of the jack-in-the-pulpit rose among the trilliums. Like the skunk cabbage, the jack-in-the-pulpit blooms before its leaves appear. It also is a plant that changes its sex, becoming female after storing up food for three or four or even five years. Another oddity among the familiar woodland flowers around us was the bloodroot. Each year it consumes the rear portion of its root and adds a new section to the front part, thus continually renewing its rootstock. Theoretically a bloodroot should be immortal. However, it requires special conditions for its existence. It dies, for instance, if the trees around it are felled.

It is no accident that most of the spring's earliest flowers bloom on the woodland floor. This is the time, before the leaves of the trees are completely unfolded and the shadows have grown dense, that the maximum amount of light for the growing season reaches the plants. Of necessity, wildflowers of the woods bloom early. Nine species of violets also grow in the glen. We saw—below the troops of trilliums, the trout lilies, and the lady-slippers—violets of many kinds: white violets, yellow violets, blue violets. During almost the whole length of our trip we found violets, like the multitudinous footprints of spring, scattered over the map before us.

Edwin Way Teale

... there are wonderful ferneries about the many misty waterfalls, some of the fronds ten feet high, others the most delicate of their tribe, the maidenhair fringing the rocks within reach of the lightest dust of the spray, while the shading trees on the cliffs above them, leaning over, look like eager listeners anxious to catch every tone of the restless waters.

John Muir

A Glen

A glen is just a narrow place
Where cool ravines may rest,
And evergreens and hardwood trees
Are nestled to her breast.

A glen may house a hundred ferns,
Or bed a spring fed brook
That sings a tumbled kind of song
Around a rocky nook.

A trail may lead along the edge
Where trillium bloom in spring,
And violets make a purple patch
Where late sun shadows cling.

A glen looks like a picture book
With air that's cool and clear.
The trees, the brook, and flowers paint
A bit of heaven there.

Mildred Perl VanHorn

In the spring, fiddleheads emerge from the ground ready to delicately uncurl into mature fern fronds.

I know of nothing in vegetable nature that seems so really to be born as the ferns. They emerge from the ground rolled up, with a rudimentary and "touch-me-not" look, and appear to need a maternal tongue to lick them into shape. The sun plays the wet-nurse to them, and very soon they are out of that uncanny covering in which they come swathed, and take their places with other green things.

John Burroughs

Fiddleheads uncurl and bright new fern fronds begin to spread themselves in the corner of the garden and on the mountainside where Dutchman's-breeches and violets are in full bloom. There is something venerable and touched with mystery in the uncurling of a fern, probably because the ferns are literally as old as the hills. Their beginnings go back millions of years. Fern fossils found in the ancient rocks show little difference from those on my own mountainside. Counterparts of lady ferns and maidenhair and wood ferns and cinnamon ferns grew here in the days when Tom's Mountain was a mud flat washed by a young, restless ocean.

For generations men were baffled by the ferns, which bore no flowers and had no visible seeds, yet throve and multiplied. They were magic plants, and those who dealt in magic believed that if only they could find the seed of the fern they would have the ultimate in mysterious power. They never found a fern "seed," of course, for ferns multiply by a complex of spores and intermediate growth in the form of prothallium, a process that takes seven years from spore to mature fern. And the process goes on so quietly and so unobtrusively that few are aware of it.

Hal Borland

The grass flames up on the hill sides like a spring fire,—as if the earth sent forth an inward heat to greet the returning sun; not yellow but green is the color of its flame;—the symbo[l] of perpetual youth, the grassblade, like a long green ribbon, streams from the soc[?] into the summer . . .

Henry David Thore[au]

Grass starts growing when snow is still on the ground but in a few short weeks the hills are again dressed in their familar lush greens.

As usual I had noted the grosser, more publicized phenomena as they appeared in their expected order. The first sound of the peepers and the first appearance of a fox sparrow were duly noted in my diary. So too was the blooming of the hepatica and, in the little wood pools, the appearance of feathery-gilled tadpoles hatched from eggs laid by a salamander a few weeks before.

But it is not these things that really change the landscape and give the whole world a new look. We await them eagerly because we know that they are points of reference; that by them we can gauge the advance of the season. But there are a thousand other phenomena no less important and far more elusive—the slow greening of the grass and the slow appearance from the ground of the thousands upon thousands of weeds and flowers.

Your peeper is either singing or he isn't; your fox sparrow is either there or not there. But who can say that he ever saw a blade of grass come up out of the ground, much less that he ever saw one of the spears which survived the winter turn green? These things do nevertheless happen, and suddenly one is aware that they have happened.

Joseph Wood Krutch

Of all the green things which make up what Goethe called "the living garment of God," grass is one of the humblest, the most nearly omnipresent, and the most stupidly taken for granted—a miracle so common that we no longer regard it as miraculous.

To some (poor things) it is merely what you try to keep the dandelions out of, or what you strike a golf ball across. But even such are paying some tribute to it. To those of us a little more aware of the great mystery of which we are a part, its going and its coming, its flourishing and its withering, are a sort of soft ostinato accompaniment in the great symphony of the seasons.

Even in the arid southwest it springs up bravely for a few short weeks. In California the brown hills turn to emerald almost overnight. And in the gentler, more circumspect east, one hardly knows when the great awakening took place. So imperceptible, but ineluctable, is its progress that those of us who watch for it never quite catch the very moment when the transformation occurs. While our backs are turned it is alive again, and no other phenomenon of spring is at once so quiet and so all-enveloping.

Joseph Wood Krutch

Grass and leaves are grateful to the eye. No other color is so restful as green. But how monotonous the earth would be if this green were not shattered again and again by the joyous exclamation of the flower! It seems to add just that touch of something more than the merely utilitarian which human beings need if they are to find life fully satisfactory. Flowers seem like a luxury that nature has grown prosperous enough to afford.

Joseph Wood Krutch

A single gentle rain makes the grass many shades greener. So our prospects brighten on the influx of better thoughts. We should be blessed if we lived in the present always, and took advantage of every accident that befell us, like the grass which confesses the influence of the slightest dew that falls on it; and did not spend our time in atoning for the neglect of past opportunites, which we call doing our duty. We loiter in winter while it is already spring. In a pleasant spring morning all men's sins are forgiven. Such a day is a truce to vice.

Henry David Thoreau

Under the Leaves

[S]have I walked these woodland paths,
Without the blessed foreknowing
[Th]at underneath the withered leaves
The fairest buds were growing.

[To]day the south wind sweeps away
The types of autumn's splendor,
[An]d shows the sweet arbutus flowers,
[S]pring's children, pure and tender,

[O] prophet-flowers!—with lips of bloom,
Outvying in your beauty
[Th]e pearly tints of ocean shells,
[Y]e teach me faith and duty!

[Wa]lk life's dark ways, ye seem to say,
With love's divine foreknowing,
[Th]at where man sees but withered leaves,
[G]od sees sweet flowers growing.

Albert Laighton

Unseen Buds

Unseen buds, infinite, hidden well,
Under the snow and ice, under the darkness, in every square or cubic inch,
Germinal, exquisite, in delicate lace, microscopic, unborn,
Like babes in wombs, latent, folded, compact, sleeping;
Billions of billions, and trillions of trillions of them waiting,
(On earth and in the sea, the universe, the stars there in the heavens,)
Urging slowly, surely forward, forming endless,
And waiting ever more, forever more behind.

Walt Whitman

Flower Chorus

Oh, such a commotion under the ground,
　　When March called "Ho, there! ho!"
Such spreading of rootlets far and wide,
　　Such whisperings to and fro!
"Are you ready?" the Snowdrop asked,
　　"'Tis time to start, you know."
"Almost, my dear!" the Scilla replied,
　　"I'll follow as soon as you go."
Then "Ha! ha! ha!" a chorus came
　　Of laughter sweet and low,
From millions of flowers under the ground,
　　Yes, millions beginning to grow.

"I'll promise my blossoms," the Crocus said,
　　"When I hear the blackbird sing."
And straight thereafter Narcissus cried,
　　"My silver and gold I'll bring."
"And ere they are dulled," another spoke,
　　"The hyacinth bells shall ring."
But the Violet only murmured "I'm here,"
　　And sweet grew the air of spring.
Then "Ha! ha! ha!" a chorus came
　　Of laughter sweet and low,
From millions of flowers under the ground,
　　Yes, millions beginning to grow.

Oh, the pretty brave things, thro' the coldest days
　　Imprisoned in walls of brown,
They never lost heart tho' the blast shrieked loud,
　　And the sleet and the hail came down;
But patiently each wrought her wonderful dress,
　　Or fashioned her beautiful crown,
And now they are coming to lighten the world
　　Still shadowed by winter's frown.
And well may they cheerily laugh "Ha! ha!"
　　In laughter sweet and low,
The millions of flowers under the ground,
　　Yes, millions beginning to grow.

Ralph Waldo Emerson

Trilliums

I know a place where trilliums grow
On the banks of a steep ravine.
To left and right they stage a show
With singing waters between.
Great oaks with fir and cedar spread
A spacious canopy overhead.

In this choice spot in early spring
Sunlight sifts through as though a dream;
Gay birds of the deep forest sing,
Soft creamy trillium blossoms gleam;
Against a setting of dark green leaves
Nature a spectrum pattern weaves.

Ablonda McBeth Koepke

Flowers of Spring

In the shadows of the forest,
Trailing through its woodland bower,
Spreads the low plant called arbutus,
With its delicate, fragrant flower.

Sharing there within its kingdom
Are trilliums and violets strewed,
Hepaticas and other wild flowers
Proclaiming spring, with life renewed.

Ernest Jack Sharpe

The flowers of spring: trillium (above); trailing arbutus (right), bladderwort (below).

The prettiest botanical specimen my trip yielded was a little plant that bears the ugly name of horned bladderwort, and which I found growing in marshy places along the shores of Moxie Lake. It has a slender, naked stem nearly a foot high, crowned by two or more large deep yellow flowers,—flowers the shape of little bonnets or hoods. One almost expected to see tiny faces looking out of them. This illusion is heightened by the horn or spur of the flower, which projects from the hood like a long tapering chin,—some masker's device. Then the cape behind,—what a smart upward curve it has, as if spurned by the fairy shoulders it was meant to cover! But perhaps the most notable thing about the flower was its fragrance,—the richest and strongest perfume I have ever found in a wild flower.

John Burroughs

How many excursions to the woods does the delicious trailing arbutus give rise to! How can one let the spring go by without gathering it himself when it hides in the moss! There are arbutus days in one's calendar, days when the trailing flower fairly calls him to the woods. With me, they come the latter part of April.

John Burroughs

Trailing Arbutus

In spring, when branches of woodbine
  Hung leafless over the rocks,
And the fleecy snow in the hollows
  Lay in unshepherded flocks,

By the road where the dead leaves rustled,
  Or damply matted the ground,
While over me lifted the robin
  His honeyed passion of sound,

I saw the trailing arbutus
  Blooming in modesty sweet,
And gathered store of its richness
  Offered and spread at my feet.

It grew under leaves, as if seeking
  No hint of itself to disclose,
And out of its pink-white petals
  A delicate perfume rose,

As faint as the fond remembrance
  Of joy that was only dreamed;
And like a divine suggestion,
  The scent of the flower seemed.

I had sought for love on the highway,
  For love unselfish and pure,
And had found it in good deeds blooming,
  Though often in haunts obscure.

Often in leaves by the wayside,
  But touched with a heavenly glow,
And with self-sacrifice fragrant,
  The flowers of great love grow.

O lovely and lowly arbutus!
  As year unto year succeeds,
Be thou the laurel and emblem
  Of noble, unselfish deeds.

Henry Abbey

The splendid rhodora now sets the swamps on fire with its masses of rich color. It is one of the first flowers to catch the eye at a distance in masses,—so naked, unconcealed by its own leaves.

Henry David Thoreau

There are many things left for May, but nothing fairer, if as fair, as the first flower, the hepatica. I find I have never admired this little firstling half enough. When at the maturity of its charms, it is certainly the gem of the woods. What an individuality it has! No two clusters alike; all shades and sizes; some are snow-white, some pale pink, with just a tinge of violet, some deep purple, others the purest blue, others blue touched with lilac.

John Burroughs

Hepatica

On a country hillside
Where the maples grow,
Flower buds are hidden
Underneath the snow.

Autumn leaves above them
Shield their fuzzy heads
While they slumber safely
In their earthy beds.

Hepatica, Hepatica,
Though wintertime is long,
Soon the breath of spring will bring
The bluebird's sweetest song.

February sunshine
Melts the crystal snow,
But above you, wildly,
Winds of March must blow
Till the April fairies
Lift your sleepy heads,
And I find you smiling
In your leafy beds.

Henrietta Staege

Hepatica

Bloodroot

Wood Violets

Bloodroot

When 'mid the budding elms the bluebird flits,
As if a bit of sky had taken wings;
When cheerily the first brave robin sings,
While timid April smiles and weeps by fits,
Then dainty Bloodroot dons her pale-green wrap,
And ventures forth in some warm, sheltered nook,
To sit and listen to the gurgling brook,
And rouse herself from her long winter nap.
Give her a little while to muse and dream,
And she will throw her leafy cloak aside,
And stand in shining raiment, like a bride
Waiting her lord; whiter than snow will seem
Her spotless robe, the moss-green rocks beside,
And bright as morn her golden crown will gleam.

E.S.F.

The violets abound now, everywhere, in the grassy fields, and among the withered leaves of the forest; many of them grow in charming little tufts, a simple nosegay in themselves; one finds them in this way in the prettiest situations possible, the yellow, the blue, and the white. A pretty habit, this, with many of our early flowers, growing in little sisterhoods, as it were; we rarely think of the violets singly, as of the rose, or the lily; we always fancy them together, one lending a grace to another, amid their tufted leaves.

Susan Fenimore Cooper

This lady's slipper is one of the rarest and choicest of our wild flowers, and its haunts and its beauty are known only to the few. Those who have the secret guard it closely, lest their favorite be exterminated.

John Burroughs

Lavender Lilacs

Have you ever breathed the fragrance
   of a lilac bush in bloom?
Then you'll not forget the pleasure
   of its dewy fresh perfume.

There were lilacs in the dooryard
   of the home where I was born.
Mother cut bouquets of lilacs
   in the coolness of the morn.

There are lilacs in my dooryard,
   planted many years ago,
By a flower-loving mother
   whose hands helped roots to grow.

Bushes of lavender lilacs,
   bouquets of fragrant perfume,
May the lilacs in the dooryards
   never cease to yield their bloom!

Jeannette K. Olson

Still grows the vivacious lilac a generation after the door and lintel and the sill are gone, unfolding its sweet-scented flowers each spring, to be plucked by the amusing traveler; planted and tended once by children's hands, in front yard plots—now standing by wall-sides in retired pastures, and giving place to new-rising forests—the last of that strip, sole survivor of that family. Little did the dusky children think that the puny slip with its two eyes only, which they stuck in the ground in the shadow of the house and daily watered, would root itself so, and outlive them, and house itself in the rear that shaded it, and grown man's garden and orchard, and tell their story faintly to the lone wanderer a half century after they had grown up and died—blossoming as fair, and smelling as sweet, as in that first spring. I mark its still tender, civil, cheerful, lilac colors.

Henry David Thoreau

The honeybee goes forth from the hive in spring like the dove from Noah's ark, and it is not till after many days that she brings back the olive leaf, which in this case is a pellet of golden pollen upon each hip, usually obtained from the alder or swamp willow. In a country where maple sugar is made, the bees get their first taste of sweet from the sap as it flows from the spiles, or as it dries and is condensed upon the sides of the buckets. They will sometimes, in their eagerness, come about the boiling place and be overwhelmed by the steam and the smoke. But bees appear to be more eager for bread in the spring than for honey; their supply of this article, perhaps, does not keep as well as their stores of the latter; hence fresh bread, in the shape of new pollen, is deligently sought for.

My bees get their first supplies from the catkins of the willows. How quickly they find them out. If but one catkin opens anywhere within range, a bee is on hand that very hour to rifle it, and it is a most pleasing experience to stand near the hive some mild April day and see them come pouring in with their little baskets packed with this first fruitage of the spring. They will have new bread now; they have been to mill in good earnest; see their dusty coats, and the golden grist they bring home with them.

When a bee brings pollen into the hive, he advances to the cell in

The flowers of spring: lady's slippers (above left); lilacs (left); crocuses visited by a pollen-seeking honeybee (above).

which it is to be deposited and kicks it off as one might overalls or rubber boots, making one foot help the other; then he walks off without ever looking behind him; another bee, one of the indoor hands, comes along and rams it down with his head and packs it into the cell as the dairymaid packs butter into a firkin.

The first honey is perhaps obtained from the flowers of the red maple and golden willow. The latter sends forth a wild, delicious perfume. The sugar maple blooms a little later, and from its silken tassels a rich nectar is gathered.

John Burroughs

Nature marches in procession, in sections, like the corps of an army. All have done much for me, and still do. But for the last two days it has been the great wild bee, the humble-bee, or "bumble," as the children call him. As I walk, or hobble, from the farmhouse down to the creek, I traverse the before-mentioned lane, fenced by old rails, with many splits, splinters, breaks, holes, etc., the choice habitat of those crooning, hairy insects. Up and down and by and between these rails, they swarm and dart and fly in countless myriads. As I wend slowly along, I am often accompanied with a moving cloud of them. They play a leading part in my morning, midday or sunset rambles, and often dominate the landscape in a way I never before thought of—fill the long lane, not by scores or hundreds only, but by thousands. Large and vivacious and swift, with wonderful momentum and a loud swelling perpetual hum, varied now and then by something almost like a shriek, they dart to and fro, in rapid flashes, chasing each other, and, little things as they are, conveying to me a new and pronounced sense of strength, beauty, vitality and movement.

Walt Whitman

In less than five minutes, the bee's pollen baskets are packed. It zooms over my head and sets a course up over the hillside to the west. For a time, I can follow the glint of its wings and body in the sun. Then it is gone. It is returning to the hive with the earliest pollen of the year, . . .

Edwin Way Teal

Magnified view of a bee's full pollen basket.

Butterflies of various colors are now more abundant than I have ever seen them before, especially the small reddish or coppery ones. I counted ten yesterday on a single *Seriocarpus conyzoides* [aster]. They were in a single harmony with the plant, as if they made a part of it. The insect that comes after the honey or pollen of a plant is necessary to it and in one sense makes a part of it. Being constantly in motion and, as they moved, opening and closing their wings to preserve their balances, they presented a very lifesome scene.

Henry David Thoreau

One of the new pleasures of country life when one has made the acquaintance of the birds is to witness the northward bird procession as it passes or tarries with us in the spring—a procession which lasts from April till June and has some new feature daily.

John Burroughs

The birds are in an ecstacy. Goldfinches, orioles, and bluebirds enliven the budding trees with their fine voices and gay plumage; wrens and songsparrows are hopping and singing about the shrubbery; robins and chipping birds hardly move out of your way on the grass and gravel, and scores of swallows are twittering in the air, more active, more chatty than ever; all busy, all happy, all at this season more or less musical. Birds who scarcely sing, have a peculiar cry, heard much more clearly and frequently at this season than any other; the twittering of the swallows, for instance, and the prolonged chirrup of the chipping bird, so like that of the locust when heard from the trees. The little creatures always enjoy a fine day extremely, but with more zest during this their honeymoon, than at any other season.

Susan Fenimore Cooper

A meadowlark sat on a fence post before me. It threw back its head and from its pulsating throat poured an ear-piercing medley of bubbling, joyous sound which spoke of spring and water and the lushness of the prairie. No sooner had it finished than another took its place, then a hundred more from every point of the compass, until there was one continuous melody, an unbroken symphony of sound. This was the theme song of the prairie.

Sigurd F. Olson

I was startled by the honking of geese flying low over the woods, like weary travelers getting in late from southern lakes, and indulging at last in unrestrained complaint and mutual consolation. Standing at my door, I could hear the rush of their wings; when, driving toward my house, they suddenly spied my light, and with hushed clamor wheeled and settled in the pond. So I came in, and shut the door, and passed my first spring night in the woods.

In the morning I watched the geese from the door through the mist, sailing in the middle of the pond, fifty rods off, so large and tumultuous that Walden appeared like an artificial pond for their amusement. But when I stood on the shore they at once rose up with a great flapping of wings at the signal of their commander, and when they had got into rank circled about over my head, twenty-nine of them, and then steered straight to Canada, with a regular *honk* from the leader at intervals, trusting to break their fast in muddier pools. A "plump" of ducks rose at the same time and took the route to the north in the wake of their noisier cousins.

Henry David Thoreau

The first sparrow of spring! The year beginning with younger hope than ever! The faint silvery warblings heard over the partially bare and moist fields from the bluebird, the song sparrow, and the redwing, as if the last flakes of winter tinkled as they fell! What at such a time are histories, chronologies, traditions, and all written revelations? The brooks sing carols and glees to the spring. The marsh hawk sailing low over the meadow is already seeking the first slimy life that awakes. The sinking sound of melting snow is heard in all dells, and the ice dissolves apace in the ponds.

Henry David Thoreau

With the first hints of spring came the brave little bluebirds, darling singers as blue as the best sky, and of course we all loved them. Their rich, crispy warbling is perfectly delightful, soothing and cheering, sweet and whisperingly low, nature's fine love touches, every note going straight home into one's heart. And withal they are hardy and brave, fearless fighters in defense of home. When we boys approached their knothole nests, the bold little fellows kept scolding and diving at us and tried to strike us in the face, and oftentimes we were afraid they would prick our eyes. But the boldness of the little housekeepers only made us love them the more.

After the arrival of the thrushes came the bobolinks, gushing, gurgling, inexhaustible fountains of song, pouring forth floods of sweet notes over the broad Fox River meadows in wonderful variety and volume, crowded and mixed beyond description, as they hovered on quivering wings above their hidden nests in the grass. It seemed marvelous to us that birds so moderate in size could hold so much of this wonderful song stuff. Each one of them poured forth music enough for a whole flock, singing as if its whole body, feathers and all, were made up of music, flowing, glowing, bubbling melody interpenetrated here and there with small scintillating prickles and spicules.

One of the gayest of the singers is the redwing blackbird. In the spring, when his scarlet epaulets shine brightest, and his little modest gray wife is sitting on the nest, built on rushes in a swamp, he sits on a nearby oak and devotedly sings almost all day. His rich simple strain is *baumpalee, baumpalee,* or *bobalee* as interpreted by some.

The sweet-voiced meadowlark with its placid, simple song of *perry-eery-ódical* was another favorite, and we soon learned to admire the Baltimore oriole and its wonderful hanging nests, and the scarlet tanager glowing like fire amid the green leaves.

But no singer of them all got farther into our hearts than the little speckle-breasted song sparrow, one of the first to arrive and begin nest-building and singing. The richness, sweetness, and pathos of this small darling's song as he sat on a low bush often brought tears to our eyes.

John Muir

The birds have started singing in the valley. Their February squawks and naked chirps are fully fledged now, and long lyrics fly in the air. Birdsong catches in the mountains' rim and pools in the valley; it threads through forests, it slides down creeks. At the house a wonderful thing happens. The mockingbird that nests each year in the front yard spruce strikes up his chant in high places, and one of those high places is my chimney. When he sings there, the hollow chimney acts as a soundbox, like the careful emptiness inside a cello or violin, and the notes of the song gather fullness and reverberate through the house. He sings a phrase and repeats it exactly; then he sings another and repeats that, then another. The mockingbird's invention is limitless; he strews newness about as casually as a god.

Annie Dillard

Two of our finest spring singers; a mother Swainson's Thrush and her young (above) and the mockingbird (below).

It threw back its head and from its pulsating throat poured an ear-piercing medley of bubbling, joyous sound which spoke of spring . . .

Sigurd F. Olson

Every evening now, the wood thrush sings. Rich and rounded, its bell tones fill those two times of half light that form the boundaries of our day. Its song, like all earthly things, contains intimations of perfection limited by imperfection. The end of the song is something of an anticlimax. The glorious notes conclude in a kind of sniffling buzz. If the end came first, if the song soared to its perfection in a triumphant climax, how much more dramatic it would be! But even so, few wild singers in the world surpass the wonderful richness of the wood thrush's finest tones as they carry through the dusky woods. We soon forget the less-than-perfect ending for the nearly perfect song.

Edwin Way Teale

Fine, clear, dazzling morning, the sun an hour high, the air just tart enough. What a stamp in advance my whole day receives from the song of that meadow lark perched on a fence stake twenty rods distant! Two or three liquid-simple notes, repeated at intervals, full of careless happiness and hope. With its peculiar shimmering-slow progress and rapid-noiseless action of the wings, it flies on a ways, lights on another stake, and so on to another, shimmering and singing many minutes.

Walt Whitman

Near at hand, upon the topmost spray of a birch, sings the brown thrasher—or red mavis, as some love to call him—all the morning, glad of your society, that would find out another farmer's field if yours were not here. While you are planting the seed, he cries, "Drop it, drop it—cover it up, cover it up—pull it up, pull it up, pull it up."

Henry David Thoreau

Nearly all the warblers sing in passing. I hear them in the orchards, in the groves, in the woods, as they pause to feed in their northward journey, their brief, lisping, shuffling, insect-like notes requiring to be searched for by the ear, as their forms by the eye. But the ear is not tasked to identify the songs of the kinglets, as they tarry briefly with us in spring. In fact, there is generally a week in April or early May, during which the piping, voluble, rapid, intricate, and delicious warble of the ruby-crowned kinglet is the most noticeable strain to be heard, especially among the evergreens.

The songless birds—why has Nature denied them this gift? But they nearly all have some musical call or impulse that serves them very well. The quail has his whistle, the woodpecker his drum, the pewee his plaintive cry, the chickadee his exquisitely sweet call, the highhole his long, repeated "wick, wick, wick," one of the most welcome sounds of spring, the jay his musical gurgle, the hawk his scream, the crow his sturdy caw. Only one of our pretty birds of the orchard is reduced to an all but inaudible note, and that is the cedarbird.

John Burroughs

...ch new year is a ...prise to us. We find ...t we had virtually ...gotten the note of ...h bird, and when ... hear it again it is ...embered like a ...am, reminding us ... previous state of ...stence. How hap-...s it that the asso-...ions it awakens ... always pleasing, ...er saddening; rem-...scences of our ...est hours? The ...ce of nature is al-...ys encouraging.

Henry David Thoreau

No sooner is one of these firstcomers seen by some member of a family, than the fact is proclaimed through the house; children run in to tell their parents, "The robins have come!" Grandfathers and grandmothers put on their spectacles and step to the windows to look at the robins; and you hear neighbors gravely inquiring of each other: "Have you seen the robins?"—"Have you heard the robins?"

Susan Fenimore Cooper

Our most welcomed and recognized migrating bird, the robin. No spring is complete without their return.

The song of the robin meant many things to me: getting up early and listening to the birds; long walks through the woods to the headwaters of trout streams with the sun bursting over the tops of trees and the underbrush sparkling with dew. It meant the sharp pungence once more of the low places at dusk, the flaming of the dogwood stems along the creeks; the reddening of the maples and the bursting of their blooms long before the leaves. It meant pussy willows in every swamp, white drifts of them against the brown of the still-frozen bogs; the Nile green that would brush the poplars and, with the pearl-gray masses of the large-toothed aspen, make each hillside and valley a pastel dream.

The robin meant the end of many things—of ski trails, and rabbit tracks, and the beds of deer in the snow. Life had changed suddenly and was full of a new excitement. From that time on I was a scout and a spy, spending every waking moment anticipating the smells, sights, and sounds of coming events.

Sigurd F. Olson

Birdsongs are not music, properly speaking, but only suggestions of music. It is as signs of joy and love in nature, as heralds of spring, and as the spirit of the woods and fields made audible, that they appeal to us.

John Burroughs

*H*yla crucifer is what the biologists call him, but to most of us he is simply the spring peeper. The popularizers of natural history have by no means neglected him but even without their aid he has made himself known to many whose only wild flower is the daisy and whose only bird is the robin. Everyone who has ever visited the country in the spring has heard him trilling from the marsh at twilight, and though few have ever caught sight of him most know that he is a little, inch-long frog who has just awaked from his winter sleep. In southern Connecticut he usually begins to pipe on some day between the middle of March and the middle of April, and I, like most country dwellers, listen for the first of his shrill cold notes.

Joseph Wood Krutch

*W*hatever the stars may say or whatever the sun's altitude may be, spring has not begun until the ice has melted and life begun to stir again. Your peeper makes a calculation which would baffle a meteorologist. He takes into consideration the maximum to which the temperature has risen, the minimum to which it has fallen during the night, the relative length of the warmer and the colder periods, besides, no doubt, other factors hard to get down in tables or charts. But at last he knows that the

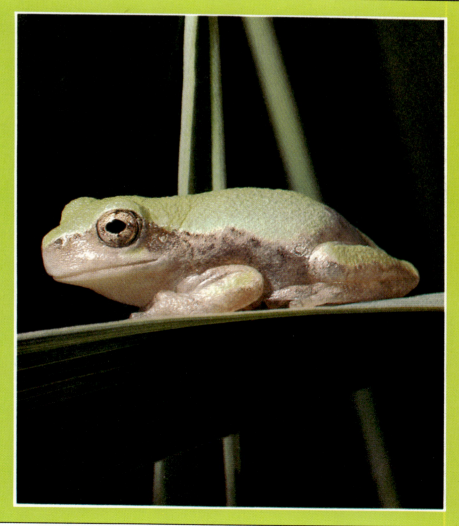

. . . the peeper seems to realize, rather better than we, the significance of his resurrection, and I wonder if there is any other phenomenon in the heavens above or in the earth beneath which so simply and so definitely announces that life is resurgent again.

Joseph Wood Krutch

moment has come. It has been just warm enough just long enough, and without too much cold in between. He inflates the little bubble in his throat and sends out the clear note audible for half a mile. On that day something older than any Christian God has risen. The earth is alive again.

Joseph Wood Krutch

Moles, feeding on earthworms, also tunnel deeper into the earth when late autumn comes and force their way upward toward the surface in the spring. Similarly, the white grubs of the May beetles burrow deeper to spend the winter below the frost-line. More than fifteen times, the periodical cicada makes such an underground migration, downward in autumn, upward in spring, before its final ascent brings it into the open air. Invisible behind the curtain of the soil, numerous earth dwellers move up and down in response to the changing seasons.

The toad, the turtle, and the frog all burrow varying distances into mud or earth for their long, cold-blooded winter sleep and work their way upward again when the spring of another year arrives. This movement is also, in its way, a vertical migration. Many fish descend into the deepest part of a lake during the months of cold. Whirligig beetles and Mayfly nymphs pull themselves downward along the stems of waterweeds at the approach of winter. And, low on forest trees, certain minute beetles creep along ridges and valleys of bark to spend the winter in the carpet of moss below. They make their way from tree trunk to moss in autumn and from moss to tree trunk in spring. Their vertical seasonal trek can be measured in inches. Yet it is truly a migration.

Edwin Way Teale

The regularity with which the chipmunks appear, with the first soft wind of spring, sets me wondering sometimes whether there is not something more than mere verbiage in the phrase, "vernal influence." Snug in their deep, dark abode, far beyond reach of sun or frost, they cannot be reached or touched by mere temperature, nor can it be that they appear at a set time, as some of our winter sleepers are said to do. No! They must come forth on the very day when first the very spring is in the land. A chipmunk announces its return to sunlight in a manner worthy of a bird. Mounted on some log or rock, it reiterates a loud chirpy "chuck-chuck-chuck." Other chipmunks run from their holes, for they awaken almost in a body, they run forth into the sunlight, and seeking some perch, add their "chuck-chuck-chuck" to the spring salute.

Ernest Thompson Seton

One attraction in coming to the woods to live was that I should have leisure and opportunity to see the spring come in . . . I am on the alert for the first signs of spring, to hear the chance note of some arriving bird, or the striped squirrel's chirp, for his stores must be now nearly exhausted, or see the woodchuck venture out of his winter quarters.

Henry David Thoreau

The first chipmunk in March is as sure a token of the spring as the first bluebird or the first robin; and it is quite as welcome. Some genial influence has found him out there in his burrow, deep under the ground, and waked him up, and enticed him forth into the light of day. The red squirrel has been more or less active all winter; his track has dotted the surface of every new-fallen snow throughout the season. But the chipmunk retired from view early in December, and has passed the rigorous months in his nest, beside his hoard of nuts, some feet underground, and hence, when he emerges in March, and is seen upon his little journeys along the fences, or perched upon a log or rock near his hole in the woods, it is another sign that spring is at hand. His store of nuts may or may not be all consumed; it is certain that he is no sluggard, to sleep away these first bright warm days.

Before the first crocus is out of the ground, you may look for the first chipmunk. When I hear the little downy woodpecker begin his spring drumming, then I know the chipmunk is due. He cannot sleep after that challenge of the woodpecker reaches his ear.

Apparently the first thing he does on coming forth, as soon as he is sure of himself, is to go courting. So far as I have observed, the love-making of the chipmunk occurs in March. A single female will attract all the males in the vicinity. One early March day I was at work for several hours near a stone fence, where a female had apparently taken up her quarters. What a train of suitors she had that day! How they hurried up and down, often giving each other a spiteful slap or bite as they passed. The young are born in May, four or five at a birth.

75

John Burroughs

At the approach of spring the red squirrels got under my house, two at a time, directly under my feet as I sat reading or writing, and kept up the queerest chuckling and chirruping and vocal pirouetting and gurgling sounds that ever were heard; and when I stamped they only chirruped the louder, as if past all fear and respect in their mad pranks, defying humanity to stop them. No you don't—chickaree—chickaree. They were wholly deaf to my arguments, or failed to perceive their force, and fell into a strain of invective that was irresistible.

Henry David Thoreau

Those creatures who cannot sing, or who do not speak our musical language when they do, communicate their joy in less direct ways. And the most eloquent of these ways is play. In some respects it is the most convincing of all the evidences of animal happiness because it demonstrates an excess of energy over and above what is required for the business of keeping alive. Those who study animals only in cages and laboratories know little about it. In prisons one must not expect to find much joy, human or animal. But the notes of field naturalists are full of accounts of the moonlight revels of rabbits and hares, of otters sliding down their chute-the-chutes into the water, of the gambols of the vixen with her young.

Joseph Wood Krutch

Those creatures w *cannot sing . . . cor* *municate their joy* *less direct ways. A* *the most eloquent* *these ways is play*

Joseph Wood K

There is always a greater love. Those who wish to pet and baby wild animals, "love" them. But those who respect their natures and wish to let them live normal lives, love them more.

Edwin Way Teale

Listen with Your Heart

Go out, go out I beg of you
    And taste the beauty of the wild.
Behold the miracle of earth
    With all the wonder of a child.
Walk hand in hand with nature's god
    Where scarlet lilies brightly flame.
Make footprints in the virgin sod,
    By some clear lake without a name.

Listen not only with your ears,
    But make your heart a listening post.
Travel above the timberline,
    Make fires on some lonely coast,
Breathe the high air of snow-crowned peaks,
    Taste fog and kelp and salty tides,
Go pitch your tent amid the pines
    Where golden sun and peace abide.

Follow the trail of moose and deer,
    The wild goose on his lonely flight,
Savor the fragrance of the wild,
    The sweetness of a northern night.
Drink deep of distance, rest your eyes
    Where centuries of peace have lain,
And let your thoughts go winging out
    Beyond the realm of man's domain.

Lay hold upon the out-of-doors
    With heart and soul and seeking brain,
You'll find the answer to all life
    Held in the sun and wind and rain.
Where'er you walk by land or sea
    The page is clear for all who seek,
If you will listen with your heart
    And let the voice of nature speak.

Edna Jaques

77

The most precious things in life are near at hand, without money and without price. Each of you has the whole wealth of the universe at your very door. All that I ever had, or still have, may be yours by stretching forth your hand and taking it."

John Burroughs

The casual glances or the admiring glances that we cast upon nature do not go very far in making us acquainted with her real ways. Only long and close scrutiny can reveal these to us. The look of appreciation is not enough; the eye must become critical and analytical if we would know the exact truth.

Close scrutiny of an object in nature will nearly always yield some significant fact that our admiring gaze did not take in.

John Burroughs

The close observation of nature, the training of the eye and mind to read her signals, to penetrate her screens, to disentangle her skeins, to catch her significant facts, add greatly to the pleasure of a walk and to life in the country. Natural history is on the wing, and all about us on the foot. It hides in holes, it perches on trees, it runs to cover under the stones and into the stone walls; it soars, it sings, it drums, it calls by day, it barks and prowls and hoots by night.

John Burroughs

If I were to name the three most precious resources of life, I should say books, friends, and nature; and the greatest of these, at least the most constant and always at hand, is nature. Nature we have always with us, an inexhaustible storehouse of that which moves the heart, appeals to the mind, and fires the imagination,—health to the body, a stimulus to the intellect, and joy to the soul. To the scientist nature is a storehouse of facts, laws, processes; to the artist she is a storehouse of pictures; to the poet she is a storehouse of images, fancies, a source of inspiration; to the moralist she is a storehouse of precepts and parables; to all she may be a source of knowledge and joy.

John Burroughs

Everywhere in the northern hemisphere spring had come and gone. The season had swept far to the north; it had climbed mountains; it had passed into the sky. Like a sound, spring spreads and spreads until it is swallowed up in space. Like the wind, it moves across the map invisible; we see it only in its effects. It appears like the tracks of the breeze on a field of wheat, like shadows of windblown clouds, like tossing branches that reveal the presence of the invisible, the passing of the unseen. So spring had spread from Georgia to North Carolina, from Virginia to Canada, leaving consequences beyond number in its wake. We longed for a thousand springs on the road instead of this one. For spring is like life. You never grasp it entire; you touch it here, there; you know it only in parts and fragments. Reflecting thus as we started south on that first morning of summer—on the day of the summer solstice, the longest day of the year—we were well aware that it is only on the calendar that spring comes to so sudden a termination. In reality its end is a gradual change. Season merges with season in a slow transition into another life.

Edwin Way Teale

"Kindred Spirits" by Durand

This is the time of year when anyone who will look and listen can't avoid the suspicion that something beyond man's restless activity is at the heart of things. The countryman plowing a field or planting corn knows that he is working with forces greater than the horsepower of his chuffing tractor, and the city person, if he looks at the grass and trees in the nearest park, knows that his meat and vegetables didn't grow there in the corner market. There's the matter of soil and sun, of the earth and the sky. There are seeds and buds, and there is germination and growth. There are urgencies and processes far older than the plow or the reaper, and they are at the root of all life as we know it. Man would perish without them.

Spring isn't really an object lesson. Nature is not in the teaching business. Nature is change and growth and all kinds of life, proceeding in its own way. But if man can't see that he is not indispensable, especially in the springtime, he is blind indeed. Grass grows, trees flourish, birds nest and animals give birth without the need of one furrow turned or one pen built. Every meadow and woodland proves it, and every treetop and riverbank.

Man gets so busy with his own affairs that he forgets. The noise he makes with his own machines tends to drown out the quiet, fundamental voices. But if all the machines rusted away, the green and quietly busy world would still be here, going about its own business. Maybe spring is a time for man to listen a few minutes, and look, and even ponder a few questions about his own omnipotence.

Hal Borland